Your
Moontime
Magic

Your Moontime Magic

A GIRL'S GUIDE TO GETTING YOUR PERIOD AND LOVING YOUR BODY

Maureen Theresa Smith

New World Library
Novato, California

New World Library
14 Pamaron Way
Novato, CA 94949

Illustrations on pages 10, 97, and 98 by Këri Bolding
Text design by Tona Pearce Myers

Library of Congress Cataloging-in-Publication data is available.

An earlier version was published as *First Moon* in 2005.
First printing of *Your Moontime Magic*, February 2020
ISBN 978-1-60868-668-1
Ebook ISBN 978-1-60868-669-8

Printed in Canada on 100% postconsumer-waste recycled paper

 New World Library is proud to be a Gold Certified Environmentally Responsible Publisher. Publisher certification awarded by Green Press Initiative.

10   9   8   7   6   5   4   3   2   1

CONTENTS

INTRODUCTION

When I was a little girl, I loved hanging out with my five older sisters. My perfect afternoon was spent sitting on their bedroom floor, a pile of their makeup spread out before me to play with, listening to them talk about all the details of their lives: their friends, their crushes, their teachers, and their favorite music. I liked to be around them as they hung out with one another, studied, made food, and got ready to go out on dates or with friends. It didn't really matter what they were doing; the fact was, they were teenage girls and I was totally fascinated with everything about them. I thought they were the coolest people ever. I liked to hear them talk about their bodies, about their relationships, and about their dreams. I loved the way they got ready to go out together, how they helped one another with their makeup and clothes, and I remember loving it when they let me braid their long hair. There was always music in the background, singing and dancing in front of the long mirror, and a lot of commotion as they prepared for a big night out. The simple ritual of getting ready was so fun that it felt like a celebration.

So much of my sisters' lives fascinated me. One of the most fascinating things was the care and comfort they offered one another during a few days of each month, and how they all seemed to feel pretty much the same way at the same time each month. I was curious about the mysterious boxes of pads and tampons tucked away in the bathroom linen closet. I was also very aware that my mother expressed an understanding that I certainly did not have. When my sisters had cramps, she would give them medicine and speak to them in a quiet and concerned voice. Though I didn't understand these things, I was acutely aware of the unspoken connection they shared. They all shared things that were still mysteries to me — a changing body and a "period," or as I now like to call it, "moon" or "moontime." I was too young to menstruate, but I felt somehow connected, knowing that I, too, would one day have a period. And somewhere inside, I felt very proud of that.

The day I got my first moon wasn't such a big deal on the outside. The truth is, I had been so eager to be part of that mysterious womanly thing that I had lied to my friends and family, telling them I had started my period a year earlier. So when I discovered a bit of blood on my school uniform skirt on my way home from school at age thirteen, I was quietly elated. But I also felt a loss: I was unable to openly share this new experience in my life and to celebrate with my mom and sisters. I wished that I could go home and tell my sisters that I was now officially "one of them." I soon realized, however, that none of my friends were celebrating the arrival of their periods either. Instead, many girls felt embarrassed or that they should hide it due to the centuries of stigma about periods. (*Stigma* means something that is looked upon as negative or to be hidden.) Isn't that ridiculous? A perfectly normal, natural biological process would be stigmatized?

Years later, in college, I studied women's history and women in many cultures. I learned some really cool things. Did you know that since the beginning of civilization, many cultures around the world have celebrated a young woman's first moon with dancing, gifts, and festivities?

For Native American girls from California coastal tribes, *menarche* (another word for the first moon or period) was an occasion for lots of attention from their families and villages. In the fall, a special dance to honor several girls' menarches brought groups of neighboring villagers, who arrived with gifts, food, and singing. The festivities lasted five days. In Brazil, a young woman's first period is celebrated with a parade of flowers. When I learned this, I thought, "That's the way to enter your womanhood!"

I have come to believe that celebrating your changing body and celebrating yourself are key to happiness, fun, and creativity in life. Celebrating with friends and family and sharing stories and traditions are part of what makes being a girl and becoming a woman so rich, full, and magical.

So this book is all about celebrating this incredible time in your life — a time when you are growing from the beautiful girl you are now into the amazing woman you were born to be. It's also about making sure you have the tools you need to create a life full of happiness, magic, and celebration for yourself. I've included lots of ways you can cultivate fun, creativity, and wisdom during your moontime and throughout your life. To help with that, you'll find these sections throughout the book:

Moontime Journaling: Prompts for things to write about in your journal to help you become all you dream of being.

Moontime Munchies: Recipes for delicious, nourishing foods you can make.

Moontime Moments: Things you can do to honor, empower, or pamper yourself during moontime.

Moontime Magic: Craft and self-care projects to adorn your home and your life.

Moontime Meditation: Practices to relax your body, quiet your mind, and spark your imagination. You can find audio versions of these on my website at www.your moontimemagic.com.

Moontime Herstory: Stories of inspiring contemporary and historical women to fuel your dreams.

Moontime Mythology: Moontime and goddess traditions from all over the world.

I hope this book helps to ensure that you have everything you need to discover and love yourself. Women are magical. You are the magic. Celebrate yourself on the special day when you have your first moon, and let every moontime cycle be a reminder to continue to celebrate and honor yourself. You are a magical, magnificent woman!

NOTE TO READERS

I wrote this book from the perspective of a cisgender female. However, the information shared is for everyone with a period or identified as a girl.

Chapter One

THE MENSTRUAL CYCLE

Preparing for Moontime

The first moon is an experience shared by women since the beginning of humankind, though your personal journey is unique to you. The nice thing is that because most women have or have had periods each month, we are united in the experience of the menstrual cycle. On the occasion of your first moon, you become part of the ever-growing and ever-changing circle of women and our personal and collective moontime magic!

I honor and celebrate you today with the following stories, exercises, and wisdom, all meant to support, nurture, inspire, and accompany you as you grow during this time of your cycle. Most important, remember that you are celebrated each and every day. Because of you, the world is a better place!

MOONTIME MYTHOLOGY
The Goddess Menses

Many girls learn about and celebrate their first moon by hearing stories about menstruation from other girls and women. Sometimes it's fun to create your own moontime myths. Here is a moontime myth created by a mom named Marge Rosenthal to explain menstruation to her two daughters.

> Once a month, the Goddess Menses visits a woman's body. She is a very mysterious goddess. Sometimes she sneaks in without us knowing, and sometimes she announces herself with powerful tuggings inside our bodies. When men bleed, it is always a sign of illness or injury, but the bleeding the Goddess Menses brings is a reaffirmation of life, a cleansing of our bodies. Her arrival is a time of celebration, a time to buy flowers or something small and special just for us women. The Goddess Menses is a high-spirited, energetic goddess who plays tricks on our bodies, arriving early or late, quiet or stormy, and tugging or rolling over us, but once her presence is acknowledged, she is very happy to settle down and wait…until next time.

WHAT HAPPENS WHEN YOU MENSTRUATE
Understanding the Basics

To best understand what is happening when you menstruate, it is important to first have a general understanding of your body. Girls and women have special organs inside and outside our bodies that developed before we were born, as we were growing inside our mothers' wombs. Now that you are growing from a girl into a young woman, these organs are beginning to develop and mature, too. These organs are generally referred to as the organs of the female reproductive system, or *genitalia*. To best learn about these special organs, you can look at the illustrations on the next page and, if you like, use a small hand mirror to look at your own body.

The organs on the outside — the parts of your body you can see just by looking between your legs — are the *external female genitalia*. A more common name for the external female genitalia is the *vulva*. The outermost part of the vulva is the outer lips, or *labia majora*. During puberty, the time when your body is changing from a girl's into a woman's, pubic hair will start to cover these outer lips. Inside or sometimes protruding from the outer lips are the inner lips, which are also called the *labia minora*. These lips might be pink or brown; they might have some blue or purple areas; and they might be larger, the same size as, or smaller than the outer lips. The inner lips might be wrinkled or smooth. All these variations are normal. Every girl is unique, and there are as many differences in the lips' size, shape, and color as there are girls in the world. Toward the top of the inner lips is the *clitoral hood*.

Just beneath it is the *clitoris*. It is a very small organ. The clitoris is filled with thousands of nerve endings that make it very sensitive and can create good physical feelings and arousal — meaning sexual feelings. It will continue to grow and become more sensitive as you develop.

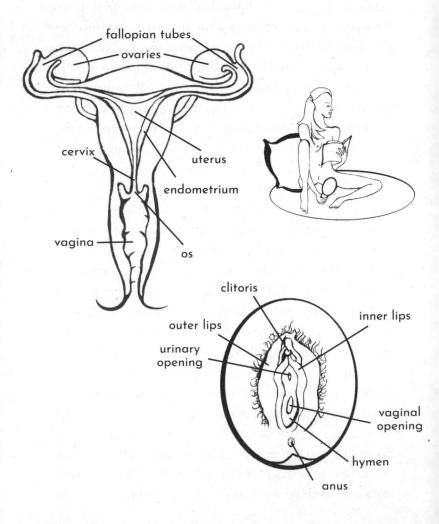

Below the clitoris is a very small opening called the *urethra*. This is where your urine passes from your bladder. Just below the urethra is the *vaginal opening*. This is the opening to the internal reproductive system and organs. In many girls, the opening is partially covered by the *hymen*, which is a thin tissue. Many other girls are born without this tissue, and the hymens of some girls have been stretched or torn from exercise. Whether you have a hymen or not, you are normal. The vaginal passageway is very important. It is a moist entryway that leads to the internal genitalia. First, it leads to the *cervix*. The cervix is small, with a little indent called the *os* in its center. The os is the opening to another small organ, the *uterus*. When a woman gives birth, this tiny opening grows large enough for a baby to pass through, but the rest of the time it stays very, very small. The uterus is hollow and has a lining of tissue called the *endometrium*. The uterus is special because it stays small except when a woman is pregnant, but then expands to hold the baby during pregnancy. Once the baby is born, the uterus shrinks back to its regular size.

Extending from the top of the uterus are two tube-like projections, the *fallopian tubes*, which connect to two small organs called *ovaries*. The ovaries produce a hormone, *estrogen*, that is responsible for your body changing from a young girl's into a young woman's. The ovaries also contain eggs, or *ova*. The ova contain each woman's genetic information, which will become part of the genetic makeup of a new baby.

Girls have approximately 250,000 eggs in their ovaries, and these begin to mature during puberty. A mature egg is released each month from an ovary and travels through one of the fallopian tubes to the uterus. This is called *ovulation*. If the egg merges with male sperm, released from a man's penis, it becomes a *fertilized* egg. It may then attach itself to the walls of the uterus, where it is nourished by the endometrium, the blood-rich tissue inside the uterus mentioned earlier. This is called pregnancy. If the egg isn't fertilized — which means there is no pregnancy — it disintegrates. The endometrial tissue, which has been building up to nourish a fertilized egg in pregnancy, also disintegrates. The tissue passes out of the body as the menstrual flow each month.

Words and Descriptions for Menstruation

Many terms are used to discuss menstruation: *menstruation*, *menses*, *menarche*, *period*, *menstrual cycle*, and my favorites, *first moon* and *moontime*. I will go through each of these terms with you so that you'll understand what people are referring to when they use the terms and to help you understand more about your body. There is also a glossary of terms in the back of this book. I'm sure you have your own words to refer to your period and vagina; this is a more clinical list.

Menarche, or first moon: *Menarche* and *first moon* are terms that describe the *first time* a young woman experiences menstruation. Menarche, or first moon, usually happens between the ages of nine and fourteen, although it can occur earlier or later. The time menarche arrives has a lot to do with your heritage — asking your mother, grandmothers, aunts, and sisters when they began their periods can give you an idea of when your first moon might occur.

Period, menses, moontime: *Period*, *menses*, and *moontime* refer to the three to seven days a month when your body releases menstrual fluid.

Menstrual flow: *Menstrual flow* is another term for menstrual fluid.

Menstruation and menstrual cycle: The terms *menstruation* and *menstrual cycle* refer to the complete, month-long process described above. Your period is the first phase of your cycle. During the second phase, your body produces more estrogen, which makes endometrial tissue grow. The third phase, *ovulation*, is when an egg is released from an ovary. In the fourth phase, your body produces another hormone, called *progesterone*, and more estrogen, which continue to grow the endometrium. If the egg isn't fertilized, the body makes less of these hormones, and the endometrial lining sheds along with a small amount of blood — and the menstrual flow or period begins again. The whole menstrual cycle usually takes approximately twenty-eight days; however, it is normal to have shorter or longer cycles. When you are just beginning to menstruate, it might be that you experience only a few periods in your first year instead of one each month, as it can take some time for your body to develop and adjust to new changes. You can keep track of your cycles on your calendar, in your journal, or on an app.

Menstruation is a healthy and normal part of life.

Menstruation happens for a very important reason: it is part of the reproductive system. Every month, your body begins to prepare itself for a possible pregnancy. Even though pregnancy is not something young girls are ready to prepare for, menstruation is how the body develops and gets ready for a possible pregnancy someday. Following the natural cycle and rhythm of menstruation can support you as you prepare for all kinds of other newness in your life: new interests, new dreams, and new visions. I will talk more about this in later chapters.

THE MOONTIME STARTER KIT:
SUPPLIES YOU WILL NEED
WHEN YOU START YOUR PERIOD

Preparing for your first moon is an easy and fun thing to do. If you have already had your first moon, then preparing for your next moontime can help make your period nurturing, stress-free, effortless, and comfortable.

Since it's hard to know when your menstrual flow will begin, the best thing to do is to create a moontime kit. The important thing to remember is that if you are not prepared, don't worry. Most women have a period. It's a natural, healthy part of life, and you will be able to get the help, advice, and supplies you need no matter where you are.

A Moontime Starter Kit Story

My middle-school friend Kali had an amazing grandmother named Mama Maria. She was from Italy and spoke with a heavy accent. During her yearly visits to see her grandchildren, she took care of Kali and her siblings while their parents worked. Maria always made sure Kali and her sisters and brothers had everything they needed as they left the house for school each day. One of the sweetest gifts Maria gave Kali was a small, beautifully decorated handmade zippered cloth case. Kali carried it in the outside pocket of her backpack. I was always curious about what was inside, but Kali was private about her bag from Mama Maria.

One day in the girls' bathroom, she asked me to get it out of her backpack for her. She let me see what was inside. The case carried a few menstrual pads (two thick pads and one thin), an extra pair of underwear, a small medicine box with a few pain-relief tablets, and a little note on red stationery from Maria to Kali that read, "Take special care of yourself today, granddaughter. Be gentle and listen to your body. Pay attention to your dreams. This is your special woman time."

I thought this was one of the sweetest gifts I had ever seen. I was also very interested in the message about paying attention to your dreams that Mama Maria had included. I had no idea why she would say this or how it was connected to having a period, but it struck me as important somehow. It was more of the moontime mystery that I had found so intriguing with my sisters. I decided I wanted to make a moontime kit for myself, and I pretended that it was from a wise and mysterious aunt, who, in my imagination, would continue teaching me the mysteries of being a woman.

You and your mom, sisters, or friends can customize a moontime supply case and include whatever you want! You can find carrying cases at most stores, usually in the toiletries section — or you can make your own. I also include some sources for period kits in the Resources section in the back of the book.

Suggested Items to Include in a Moontime Kit

1. A reminder just for you: This could be a nice note to yourself, a special stone, or jewelry that reminds you to take special care of yourself today.
2. Two or three pads (thick and/or thin, depending on how heavy or light your flow is).
3. An extra pair of underwear (in case you leak).
4. A few pain-relief tablets (with your doctor's and parent's permission).
5. Body oil or massage oil infused with essential oils to massage onto cramped areas, or Magical Moontime Mist (see pages 88–89) to breathe in the soothing scents.
6. If you're expecting your very first moon, include a "get out of school free" card just for this first day. This gives you permission to call your mom, dad, or guardian to pick you up if you need to be home or to do something special for yourself today.

If you are uneasy about the possibility of getting your period at school, you could also pack a sweatshirt or an extra pair of jeans or shorts in your backpack. You will probably feel the menstrual fluid long before it reaches your outer clothes, but if it does soak through, it usually will be a very small amount that can be easily covered by tying a sweatshirt around your waist. When I had my first period, I was walking to the bus stop, wearing my school uniform skirt. A little fluid did leak onto my skirt, but I was able to wrap my sweatshirt around my waist until I got home.

TAMPONS, PADS, AND MORE: MAKING SENSE OF YOUR OPTIONS TO PICK WHAT'S BEST FOR YOU!

For thousands of years, women have used all kinds of things to catch their menstrual flow — from tree moss to leaves to cloth rags to modern pads and tampons. Many choices are available to girls and women today. They are advertised as *feminine hygiene products* or *menstrual protection products*. With so many choices, you are free to experiment and select the products that work best for you.

Living in a house full of big sisters, I was aware that there were all kinds of products for girls to choose among when they got their periods. Sometimes I would spend time alone or with my best friend sitting on the bathroom floor, secretly reading all the instructions and looking at the diagrams and illustrations that came with the pads or tampons. I wanted to figure it all out — periods, my body, how it would work — and I also wanted to be sure that I knew what the best products were. I also wanted to use what seemed "coolest" or most advanced or trendy. What I discovered, when I finally did get my period, was that there is no one "cool" product. I liked to use both tampons and pads, in different sizes and styles, at different times during my period. Some of my preferences have changed over time as my own life, body, and needs have changed. When it comes to being cool, cool means what works best for you. If you feel comfortable, secure, and good, then you are happy. And that's cool.

Another way to figure out which products are best for you is to choose a certain type or brand of tampon or pad. This might be the first time you make a decision about how you wish to spend your money as a consumer of products made just for women. You will now have many opportunities to consider which women's items you want to buy. Your awareness and personal values might grow as you think about what is important to you when you spend your money. For example, when I was a young woman, I did not know about products that were better for the environment and my body than others, products labeled "environmentally safe" or "biodegradable" or "organic." But, just as I have learned over time about the importance of taking good care of my body, I have also learned about an important responsibility: to care for Earth's body. Now I am aware that I can purchase organic tampons. It is important to me to use products that are not harmful to the environment or my body. Products free of chemicals and products that biodegrade disintegrate over time and do not create waste. Whenever possible, I choose to buy organic, environmentally safe products. When you're choosing the right menstrual products for you, these issues might also be important for you to consider.

There are several types of products on the market, and new ones appear all the time. Following are general descriptions and tips on the products I know best; however, you might find other types that are not listed here. Feel free to peruse the shelves in the feminine hygiene section, take your time reading labels, and never be embarrassed to purchase the supplies you need. I recommend a swapping spree with friends. You might want to try out each type of product to discover for yourself which products you like best. You can also ask your mom and your friends which products they like best and why. I have provided a list of resources that includes helpful websites and information on feminine hygiene products at the back of this book.

All about Pads

Pads offer a soft, thick layer of material for absorbency. They come in different sizes, and many have adhesive "wings" designed to protect your panties. Here are some descriptions of the different types of pads to choose from:

Minipads (small and used for light flow) and **maxipads** (thick and used for heavy flow) are easy to use. Both kinds have adhesive tape on the bottom side of the pad that sticks on to your underwear. Maxipads are best for a heavy flow and can provide extra protection overnight. Some girls need to change their pads several times a day, others just a couple of times, depending on their flow.

Pads with wings are made to further protect your panties and prevent staining. Generally, however, I find that when I have my period, I do get some blood on my underwear during the first couple of days.

Reusable cotton pads are an option, especially if you are seeking comfort and environmental consciousness. As Lynda Madaras points out in *The "What's Happening to My Body?" Book for Girls*, women in the United States use approximately 12 billion menstrual pads each year. If you were to lay them end to end, the pads would stretch 1.6 million miles. That's enough for three round-trips to the moon! Seven billion tampons go into landfills, sewers, and waterways every year. Cotton pads are both comfortable and nonpolluting. You can soak a used pad in water and then launder it in the washing machine. Many companies sell airtight carrying cases for used pads. Like other pads, these come in different shapes, sizes, and styles. You can find them at most health-food stores or online.

Panty liners are very thin pads and not as useful as thicker pads during your period, but they can come in handy on light-flow days as your period tapers off. Some women like to use them to protect their panties during other times of the month if they experience a lot of *vaginal discharge* (a clear or whitish fluid that is released between periods, especially during ovulation).

All about Tampons

Tampons are another option for absorbing menstrual blood. A tampon is different from a pad in that it is used inside the vagina. It is a small cotton tube or plug with a string hanging from one end. Some brands have a plastic or cardboard applicator for inserting the tampon, and some are designed to be inserted with your finger. A tampon is inserted into the vagina to absorb the blood before it leaves the vagina. Once it has absorbed all that it can hold (usually after four hours), you take the tampon out by pulling the string.

Tampons cannot get lost or go "too far" into the vagina. As mentioned above in the description of the reproductive system, the cervix is very small, too small for a tampon to fit through. After a tampon is used, it should be wrapped in toilet paper and thrown away (not flushed).

Depending on the lightness or heaviness of your flow, you might need different sizes of tampons (super for heavy flow, light or regular for light flow), as with pads. Tampons are especially useful if you plan to swim or engage in athletic activities, when you don't want menstrual blood to leak. Many companies sell organic cotton tampons and tampons with biodegradable applicators.

Important Safety Information about Tampons

If you aren't sure about the right time to begin using tampons, it's a good idea to check with your parent(s) and/or your doctor. Here are some other important things to know about the safe and effective use of tampons.

Every tampon box contains a warning about toxic shock syndrome (TSS). TSS is a rare illness that occurs when bacterial toxins from the vagina enter a girl's or a woman's bloodstream, causing her to become very sick or, in some extremely rare cases, causing death. Symptoms of TSS include fever, vomiting, diarrhea, lightheadedness, aching muscles, headaches, and a rash that looks like a sunburn. It is an illness that progresses quickly, but it can be treated effectively if caught early. TSS can develop when tampons are used, especially if they are not used correctly. If you or anyone you know experiences these symptoms while using a tampon, it is important to remove the tampon and call a doctor.

The best method for preventing TSS is to use the smallest size of tampon necessary to absorb your flow. This could mean using different sizes over the course of your period. Another important practice is to change your tampon frequently, waiting no longer than every two to four hours. A healthy approach to preventing TSS is to use pads as often as possible, particularly at night.

Other Products to Consider

Menstrual cups are a great option as well! They are small reusable cups, usually made out of silicone, which is similar to rubber. You can insert one into your vagina to hold period blood, then you remove it over a toilet. Clean it out, and it's ready to be used again. Using them can be a bit strange at first (like using a tampon), but once you get the hang of it (and cleaning it out), you might appreciate that it's super Earth-friendly and much less costly.

Period underwear is another option to consider. Basically, they're underwear that have an absorbent pad built in. You can wear them and no longer worry about leaking and staining your clothes. There are even swimwear styles now available.

Essential oils (which I discuss further in chapter 5) can be extremely soothing during moontime. Some of my favorites to soothe cramps are Roman chamomile and lavender. You can place a washcloth under warm water, apply a few drops of the oils, and place it on your lower abdomen. Or just add them to a bath and soak. Essential oils can be found at your local health-food store or on-line.

Personal Preferences

After I had my first moon, I used pads for the first few months. This gave me a chance to learn about my menstrual flow and its rhythm. By the time summer came around, I wanted to be able to swim, and I was ready to try tampons. I started with a "slender" or "junior" size that is made specifically to be comfortable for a young woman trying tampons for the first time. I asked two of my girlfriends to demonstrate how to use a tampon. Once they had shown me, we showed another friend. It seemed tricky at first. Instructions are included with a tampon box, but it was really helpful — and pretty funny — to learn from my friends. It was a bonding experience that illustrated the importance of having girlfriends!

GOOD WAYS TO TAKE GOOD CARE: FRIENDS, STORIES, AND ADVICE

"Going Green" by Fiona, 16

When I learned about organic tampons and reusable cotton pads, I started using them because I wanted to do my part to protect the environment. Cotton pads are very soft and comfortable. I like the way they feel more than regular pads, and I like the benefit to the environment. I didn't like having to soak and wash them at first — it seemed inconvenient and kind of gross — but after a while, I started liking them because I feel so much better about being a woman and taking care of my body and the Earth.

"Naps and Comfort" by Mary, 14

When I first started getting my periods, I took lots of naps because I thought that way I'd have less time to spend actually, consciously *having it*. I got my period really young, and I wasn't quite ready for the whole growing-up thing yet.

Oh, and *leggings*! I don't even bother with jeans during that time of the month. I just let myself stretch out and feel comfy.

"Why I Love Tampons" by Wende, 36

When I first got my period, in sixth grade, my mom gave me a pad. Then my friend invited me to go swimming, so I asked my mom how I would do that, and she said,

"You don't." So I went with a pad but couldn't go in the pool. The other girls kept asking me why I wouldn't go in, and when I finally told them, one said, "Why don't you use a tampon?" I didn't even know what they were, and it would take me another three years to figure them out!

Finally, in ninth grade, I met this girl that I really liked. One of the first ways we bonded was by learning that we were both afraid to put tampons in — so we decided to help each other figure it out. That summer, we happily hit the beach and learned to surf!

MOONWEAR

Most of my friends have a pile of raggedy undies stashed away in their underwear drawers that they save to use during their periods. But I suggest treating yourself to seven pairs of ultra-comfortable cotton panties just for your moontime. That way, you have super-comfy, stain-acceptable panties for your moontime, and you can save your other, favorite undies for the rest of the month.

 ### MOONTIME MAGIC
Decorate Your Own Moonwear

Start a fashion trend among your girlfriends by designing your own moonwear. Here's how:

1. Start with a little shopping. First, purchase five to seven pairs of comfy 100 percent cotton (or even better, 100 percent organic cotton) underwear.

2. Next, purchase some fabric paint and paint fixative. Both are readily available at crafts stores or online and come with directions for use. They are super-affordable and easy to use. You might also find some cool iron-ons.

3. Wash and dry your new panties.

4. Set up a space in your home where you can be creative. Lay some newspaper down to protect the surface you are working on. Be sure it is fully covered so that it's safe from paint stains.

5. Add a bit of fixative to your paint, according to the label directions, to prevent the paint from running in the washing machine later.

6. Go for it! Design the moonwear of your dreams. Paint the phases of the moon or a sprinkling of stars; write the word *MOON* or the days of the week across the back of your undies. (Did you know that *Monday* means "Moon-day"?)

7. Let dry for seven days.

8. Wash inside-out and line-dry. (It is always best to line-dry clothing that has been treated with fabric paint.) Enjoy!

PADS AND TAMPONS

Education, Empowerment, and Freedom!

In some parts of the world, menstruation is still very stigmatized. We know that periods are completely normal and natural — but in some places they are still misunderstood. For generations in a rural village outside Delhi, India, girls and women haven't had access to pads, which leads not only to health problems but even to girls missing school or dropping out entirely! Can you imagine having to stop your education because you did not have access to pads or feel comfortable even talking about your period?

In 2018 the documentary *Period. End of Sentence*, directed by Rayka Zehtabchi, won the Academy Award for best short documentary. The film tells the story of the girls and women in this village fighting against this stigma. To address the problem, Arunachalam Muruganantham, a local man, invented a machine that makes menstrual pads from locally sourced materials. He taught the women in the village to use the machine to make these affordable, biodegradable pads for other women, and it has changed their lives. The women learn to manufacture and sell their own pads — empowering themselves and the other women in their community. They even named their brand "FLY" because they want women to soar! Their journey has been, in part, enabled by the work of high school girls half a world away, in California, who raised the initial money for the machine and began a nonprofit called the Pad Project.

As the Pad Project website says: "A period

should end a sentence, not a girl's education. But, unfortunately, that's exactly what's happening all over the world.... There is a new invention that solves this problem." If you want to learn more about this work, visit the Pad Project at www.the padproject.org.

Chapter Two

CELEBRATION

Honoring Your First Moon

I celebrate your passage into young womanhood. Because of you, the world is a better place. The Navajo believe that at the time of menarche a young woman brings gifts to her people and that everything she touches is blessed with her womanhood. Your first moon is a magical time. By celebrating your first moon in a way that is special to you, you can love and honor the amazing girl you are.

CELEBRATING TRANSITIONS

Changes and transitions, times when you are growing from one phase of your life into the next, are parts of life that we can always count on. Sometimes they are easy, and other times they are not so easy. All kinds of feelings can be attached to transitions. Sometimes you might feel really excited about growing up. Other times you might hate it and want to stay a kid forever. You might like your changing body but also feel awkward and not quite comfortable in it yet. You might like the idea that your body is beginning to change into a beautiful womanly shape, but you might also miss your kid shape. Your first moon signifies this time of change in your life. It's a time to celebrate your kid self, your between-kid-and-woman self, your entering-into-womanhood self — and all the feelings and dreams that come with them.

Celebrating your first moon might be one of many celebrations of passages in your life, and it might be the first of many "in-between" stages, too. For thousands of years, in cultures all over the world, a young woman's first moon has been seen as such an important time in her life that special celebrations and festivities mark this moment of growth, beauty, and change. Celebrate yourself today! You are a beautiful and amazing girl.

 MOONTIME MYTHOLOGY
A Navajo Celebration

The Navajo people celebrate the connection between a girl's first moon and succeeding passages in her life, like childbirth and old age. During her puberty ceremony, the girl is dressed in the image of Changing Woman, the most powerful Navajo deity. She wears beautiful, colorful clothing and is decorated with turquoise jewels. Turquoise is Changing Woman's sacred stone and is associated with the Earth. As the girl is dressing, a song of honor and celebration is sung to her by the women in her tribe. The song tells her of the treasured jewel she is for herself and her people. The association with Changing Woman reminds the girl that her life is always changing and in transition, and that there are many phases of life.

GIRLS AND MOMS SHARE THEIR MOONTIME EXPERIENCES

Celebrating your first moon in a way that is just right for you is important. There are many, many possibilities. Some girls like to go out to lunch and spend an afternoon shopping with their mom or "other mom" (an "other mom" is any trusted adult woman in your life whom you can share things with); others might like to invite a circle of women and girlfriends over for a first-moon ritual celebration. Still others might see their first-moon celebration as tying in well with another coming-of-age ceremony or ritual, such as a bat mitzvah or confirmation.

Keri's Story

Keri decided she wanted to celebrate by having a slumber party with four of her girlfriends, her mom, and her aunt. They made a special "moontime meal" together. The table was beautifully set with candles, flowers, Keri's favorite foods, and wish boxes. The girls each took turns writing their wishes for Keri and placing them in her wish box. Then they wrote wishes for themselves and filled their own. For dessert, they created a "wish cake" borrowed from another family tradition. Hidden in the cake were three silver dollars representing the wealth and gifts of Keri's dreams. After dinner, the girls and women each told stories about their first moons and how girls can care for themselves during their moontime. They painted their nails, ate good food, and giggled late into the night. Keri loved feeling celebrated and supported by the girls and women in her life.

MEDITATING ON MOONTIME

In India, when girls of the Nayar culture have their first moon, they sit in seclusion to meditate on their new womanly status before they are dressed in a new sari by their female neighbors, taken to a ceremonial bath, and given a feast. You might like to try meditation for yourself at this special time.

What Is Meditation?

Some people say that meditation is the best way to become best friends with yourself! Meditation is a way to give yourself a time-out from the world, tune in to your own thoughts and feelings, calm down, and feel good. It's a simple way to relieve stress and tension, be comfortable in your body, balance your emotions, and easily revive your energy and creativity. It's also a way to get quiet and just be. Meditating at the time of your moon — and during other times of change — is an easy and fun way to take good care of yourself. It is a practice that people in many cultures have used for centuries to help themselves relax and find internal calm, no matter what is going on in the external world. It is a way to bring good things into your life by taking time to appreciate what you have today and to imagine how you would like your life to be and how you want to feel.

 ## MOONTIME MEDITATION
A First-Moon Celebration

The following is what's called a *guided meditation* or *guided imagery*. *Guided* means that you read or listen to a story while you're really relaxed and let your imagination follow along. Its only difference from reading a regular story is that you can use it to gain more insight into your own thoughts and feelings.

Before you begin, you might want to ask your mom, dad, another family member, or a woman friend to read this to you as you relax with your eyes closed. Or you could make an audio recording of yourself reading it very slowly before you begin. You can also listen to the recording I have made available to you through my website: www.yourmoontimemagic.com. If you can't do any of these things, read through the meditation first, then lie down and imagine it in your mind, taking your time.

When you are ready, find a comfortable place to relax, lying down flat or sitting up with your eyes closed. Take a few deep breaths. Feel your chest rise and fall with your breath. With each exhalation, imagine all your thoughts and worries from the day leaving your body. As you breathe in, imagine that your body is filled with warmth, love, and calm.

Imagine yourself walking down a beautiful forest path. It is an enchanting moonlit night. You have no trouble seeing because the full moon is so bright that it lights the path for you to follow. Your closest friends surround you. In the near distance you hear other girls and women singing. As you walk toward this sound, you are filled with anticipation and excitement. The singing gets closer and closer. Just in front of you, you see a clearing lit by the full moon.

As you walk into the clearing, two girls, who are just a year or so older than you, greet you and your friends. They hand you beautiful flowers and place a crown of flowers on your head. Taking your hands, they guide you into the center of a circle made up of many girls and women. As you look around, you see the faces of women from every part of the world, of all ages, singing you a beautiful song of celebration and welcome. You realize that even though each woman sings in her native language, together their voices are in perfect harmony and the words make perfect sense to you. The music is so beautiful and you are so happy that you and the other girls and women start to dance. Looking around at all the women in the circle with you, you begin to see your connection to them and your connection to the Earth, the moon, and the stars. As the singing ends, your eyes fall on one of the women.

Her gaze meets yours, and she smiles. She has a special gift for you. Her gift is from all the women in the circle. It contains the wisdom shared by all women for all ages. She comes to you and offers you the special gift. Take time now to receive your gift. Imagine that it is words, a symbol, or a song — and whatever it is, it is just for you. Take your gift to your heart. Place your hands over your heart. This is your welcome into the greater circle of women. This circle is always here for you. It is your own special place to come and receive wisdom and understanding anytime you might need it in your life. This circle lives in your heart. Allow yourself time to rest here, listening to anything else the woman or women have to say.

When you are ready, imagine looking up to the sky to see the moonlight disappearing and the dawn of the new day arriving. This new day begins a new phase of your life. You are filled with happiness, love, and strength. You know that you are never alone and that you have generations of women to love, support, and assist you as you grow.

And now begin to bring your awareness back to today, carrying with you your gift and memories from this special celebration. Remember that you can return to this circle of women's wisdom whenever you need to, just by asking and touching your heart.

And when you feel ready, wiggle your toes, take a deep breath, and open your eyes.

JOURNALING DURING MOONTIME

I invite you to make a personal moontime journal to use as you read this book. You can use a blank notebook or special journal from a bookstore. Decorate it with stickers or colored pens — make it your own. You can write about anything you like in it. Some girls use their journals to record their daily thoughts and the events of the day. Some girls think of their journals as good friends who listen to all their thoughts, feelings, dreams, and fears, and they can write anything in their journals without any fear of judgment or worry that someone else might hear their words.

Journaling can be especially fun because during your moontime, you might often find that your dreams are more vivid or easier to remember, or because you might feel especially reflective or creative and want a place to write. It might also be a place where you can start to record all kinds of other stuff: your moontime meditation experiences, your own moontime stories and myths, details about the way your body feels during your cycle or what kinds of food you eat — things that you notice help you feel good during your moontime.

MOONTIME JOURNALING
Reflections

1. Take out your moontime journal. Write about your first-moon celebration meditation. What was it like? How did you feel? What friends and

women did you recognize in your meditation? What (if any) gifts were you given? Did you like the experience? Is meditation something you would like to try again?

2. List ten things that you like about yourself. Then acknowledge and celebrate these special qualities by hanging a copy of the list on your mirror so you can see it each day — and keep adding to the list!

PLANNING YOUR FIRST-MOON CELEBRATION

How would you like to celebrate your first moon? (And if you have already had your first moon but did not really celebrate, you can always do so now!) Would you like a special dinner? A ceremony with friends and family? To shop for something special that's just for you? Take out your journal and write about what you would like. Then share your celebration wish with your mom, other mom, or girlfriends. It's nice to have at least one older woman around, someone who has already had the experience of her period, so that she can help you celebrate as well as answer any questions you might have.

The best thing about this celebration is that it is all for you, and you get to ask for exactly what you want. You might want to have a dinner party with a few special girls and women, such as your friends or your aunts, sisters, mom, and grandmothers. Or you might like the idea of an adventurous full-moon hike with your dad, mom, and friends.

Another great way to celebrate is to have a first-moon celebration ritual. First-moon rituals or coming-of-age ceremonies are created to acknowledge and celebrate this important time of growing from a girl to a woman. Rituals may include objects like candles, flowers, and stones that hold symbolic meaning to you and your family: a candle representing warmth and light, flowers mirroring your beauty and growth, a stone symbolizing the Earth.

Rituals give family members and friends an opportunity to show their love for you and remind you of the great circle of support that surrounds you as you grow.

What do you want your ritual to be like? As you think about what to include, ask your family and friends for their ideas. Maybe you want to dress up in a bright-red dress and adorn yourself with flowers and jewelry. Maybe you want to stand in the center of a circle and receive good wishes from your family and friends. You could bring some items into the circle with you that represent different phases of your life, such as a rattle from when you were an infant, your stuffed animal from toddler years, a trophy from your first soccer tournament, or some photographs. You could also bring a description of the woman you are seeking to become. It is a powerful experience to acknowledge the different phases of your life while surrounded by the people who love you, and to voice your dreams to these witnesses. In doing so, your dreams are born and held in the safe circle of your friends and family, and as their love nurtures you, your dreams are able to come to life.

MUNCHIES DURING MOONTIME

Moontime is a time to eat healthy foods and really nourish your body. It is also a time when some girls experience cravings for salty foods or chocolate. In chapter 3, I'll talk about nutrition and moontime body care. But for your moontime celebration, it might be fun to try a special "goody" recipe. Maybe your celebration could include baking with your mom and your friends. Below is a delicious and fun recipe for one of my favorite treats. But first, take note of these basic kitchen safety rules, and be sure to follow them.

Kitchen Safety Tips

1. Check with your parent(s) before starting a cooking project.
2. Get clean! Be sure to wash your hands. If you have long hair, tie it back.
3. Beware of germs: Raw eggs, fish, and meat can contain harmful ones. Thoroughly wash cutting boards, knives, and other cooking utensils in hot, soapy water after each use. And don't eat raw dough that contains eggs, as you could get sick.
4. Ask for help until you're more experienced in the kitchen; adults can help out with knives and electrical appliances. Make sure an adult is around when you're lighting matches, dealing with a hot oven, or cooking on a range.
5. Be careful never to touch an electrical appliance

when your hands are wet, as you could get an electric shock.

6. Make sure pot handles are turned in, toward the middle of the stove, and do not point out, toward the edge. Someone walking by could bump the handle and accidentally knock the pot off, scalding herself or someone else.

7. Use pot holders to protect your hands from burns when placing something in the oven or taking it out.

8. Use a timer and remove cooked items promptly.

9. Stay close to things cooking on the stove, so that they don't boil over. Turn off the stove burners and oven when you are finished.

10. Clean up as you go. If you spill anything, clean it up immediately. It saves you from having to clean up a giant mess at the end, when all you really want to do is eat the goodies you've made.

Have fun! It feels so great to enjoy your cooking creations and to see other people enjoying them, too.

MOONTIME MUNCHIES
Many Moons Red Velvet Cupcakes

These cupcakes are a perfectly delicious addition to your celebration! Set up your prep area with two or three mixing bowls, a whisk, an electric mixer, a big spoon, a spreading knife, a muffin tray, and cupcake wrappers. Also, you'll need to take the butter, eggs, and cream cheese out of the fridge an hour or two ahead of time to get them to room temperature. If you don't have buttermilk, you can make your own by adding a tablespoon of distilled white vinegar to milk and letting it stand for about 10 minutes. And if you don't have cake flour, you could try it with all-purpose flour and see what happens!

Cupcake Ingredients

½ cup (1 stick) butter, room temperature

1½ cups sugar

2 eggs, room temperature

2⅓ cups cake flour

2 tablespoons Dutch-processed cocoa powder

1 teaspoon baking soda

1 teaspoon baking powder

½ teaspoon salt

1 cup buttermilk

1 teaspoon distilled white vinegar

1 teaspoon vanilla extract

1½ tablespoons red food coloring

Frosting Ingredients

½ cup butter (1 stick), room temperature

8 ounces (1 package) cream cheese, room
    temperature

1 teaspoon vanilla extract

2 to 3 cups powdered sugar

To Make the Cupcakes

1. Preheat the oven to 350 degrees. Beat the butter and sugar in an electric mixer for 3 minutes on medium speed until light and fluffy.
2. Add the eggs, one at a time, beating until each is fully incorporated. Be sure to scrape down the sides of the bowl to ensure even mixing.
3. In a large bowl, sift together the cake flour, cocoa powder, baking soda, baking powder, and salt. In another bowl, whisk together the buttermilk, vinegar, vanilla extract, and red food coloring.
4. A little at a time, add the sifted dry ingredients to the wet and mix until smooth and thoroughly combined.
5. Scoop the batter into the cupcake papers, until each one is about half or three-quarters full. Bake for 10 minutes, then rotate the pan to ensure even baking. Bake another 8–12 minutes or until a toothpick comes out clean.
6. Allow the pan to cool for ten minutes, then transfer the cupcakes to a wire rack to cool completely.

To Make the Frosting

1. Beat the butter and cream cheese together, about 3 minutes. Scrape down the sides and bottom of the bowl to ensure even mixing.
2. Mix in the vanilla extract.
3. Add 2 cups of the powdered sugar and mix thoroughly. Taste the frosting. If it's not sweet enough, add a bit more sugar, and taste again. Keep going

until you get to your desired sweetness. Spread the frosting onto the cooled cupcakes.

MOONTIME MOMENTS
Changing Woman

Celebrate your first moon by dressing up in beautiful clothes. Wear something with a moon on it, like a necklace or anklet, which you can make in the Moontime Magic project below. Draw a small crescent moon and star on your cheek, or paint moons on your fingernails.

MOONTIME MAGIC
Adorn Yourself with Jewels

Create a piece of beautiful moontime jewelry, put it on, and feel how beautiful and magical you are!

Beaded Necklace, Bracelet, or Anklet

If you do not have all the supplies at home, you can find them at any crafts store or bead shop. For a special touch, include one or two charms, such as a moon, butterfly, heart, or your initial.

Supplies
Necklace wire or fishing line
Scissors or pliers
A set of necklace clasps (optional)

Your favorite beads, in any shape, size, or color
Charms (optional)

First, carefully cut the fishing line or necklace wire to the length that you need. You might want to make a long necklace, a short necklace, or maybe a bracelet or anklet. Be careful when measuring, and be sure to leave an extra 6 inches so that you can easily attach the clasps at the end of your beading. (If you make a long necklace, you won't need to use clasps, as you can just fit the necklace over your head, so you could even use ribbon, yarn, twine, or other materials instead of wire or line.)

Tie a knot in one end of the wire or line and, using the pliers, attach one of the clasps to it. Leave 2 to 3 inches of wire or line at the end, below the clasp and knot. Make sure the knot and clasp are large enough that the beads will not slip over them and fall off when you string them.

Now you can start beading. Use your imagination: you can create patterns or use beads in your favorite colors. You can use different sizes or combinations of beads. This is your special, beautiful beading creation.

Once you are finished beading, tie a knot at the other end of the line, as close to the beads as possible. Make sure it is secure. Attach the other necklace clasp. Then cut off the extra wire or line on both ends. Wear it with pride!

For thousands of years, women from all over the world have recognized the special time of the first moon. As you grow from a girl into a young woman, your body, mind, and spirit will experience many awesome changes.

Throughout your life, you will continue to experience transition and change. If you treat yourself with extra care and ceremony during this first moon, it will give you strength and confidence throughout your life and during other times of change. Mark this time of your life with fun, happiness, love, and celebration.

ACTIVISM HAVING AN IMPACT!

Over the past few years, there has been a growing movement around empowering girls with easy access to period products, know-how, and positivity, known as "menstrual equity." The phrase was coined by Jennifer Weiss-Wolf, vice president for development at the Brennan Center for Justice and author of *Periods Gone Public: Taking a Stand for Menstrual Equity*.

Research from the Always Confidence & Puberty Study in 2017 found that 1 in 5 girls in the US have missed school due to lack of period products. Menstrual movers and shakers such as Weiss-Wolf and Nadya Okamoto who cofounded PERIOD (see pages 108–9), are working to change this through their writing and activism, making the case that period products should not be taxed and should be considered a necessity.

The menstrual equity movement is having an impact, but there is still a ways to go! Advocacy organizations such as PERIOD (www.period.org), Period Equity (www.periodequity.org), Human

Rights Watch (www.hrw.org), Global G.L.O.W. (globalgirlsglow.org), and the Homeless Period Project (www.homelessperiodproject.org) are working. Let's be sure to do our part to keep the movement strong so that every girl has the products and support she needs to go to school during her moontime confident and strong!

Chapter Three

REDEFINING PMS

"Preparing Myself to Shine"

We need to learn how to nurture ourselves, each other, and the planet. One way girls and women can begin to do this is to just allow themselves some time, even an hour or two each month, to do something that deeply nurtures them.

— **Shinan Barclay,** author of
Flowering Woman: Moontime for Kory

 MOONTIME MYTHOLOGY

A Southern Ute Native American
Moontime Story

A long time ago, women did as they do now — they held the family. They held the power (life force) of the family; they held its happiness and joy; they held its sorrow and disappointments. As time passed, the negative emotions and heartache that the women took upon themselves on behalf of their families began to weigh them down. The

47

women became sick and, finally, could no longer take on the burdens of the family. Yet the Creator had given them the nature to do so.

One day, a woman was out in the forest, crying because the burden had become so great, when Raven heard her and asked, "Mother, why do you cry?"

The woman responded, "I love my family so very much. I hold my family in my heart and soul, but the pains of life have filled me up. I can no longer help my family. I can no longer take their burdens from them. I just don't know what to do."

Raven responded, "I understand the pain you feel, as I feel it also. I will go and ask Grandmother Ocean if she knows what to do." So Raven flew to the ocean and shared with Grandmother the plight of the women.

Grandmother Ocean responded, "If the women will come to me, I will wash their pain from them, but this won't help the ones who are far away. Let me ask my sister, Grandmother Moon, if she can help."

So Grandmother Ocean spoke to her sister of the women's plight. Grandmother Moon responded, "I am the power of the feminine. I will send your waters, carrying my power, into the women, my sisters. Once every moon cycle, you shall come into the women through me and purify them." And she did this.

So, ever since then, every woman has a time in each moon cycle when she embodies the power of the moon and the cleansing ocean flows through her. We call this the woman's time of the moon, or moontime.

WHAT IS PMS?

Premenstrual syndrome (PMS) usually occurs at some point during the two weeks before the first day of your period. Symptoms can include feeling tired or grumpy or having mood swings; feeling bloated (a heavy or swollen feeling in your lower belly) and/or having tender breasts; or skin blemishes, acne, headaches, and cramping, as well as increased sensitivity to feelings, smells, and sounds. Some women never experience any of these symptoms, others experience a few symptoms, and still others experience all of them. There might also be other PMS experiences — not all of them negative — than those on this general list.

It is not clear exactly what causes PMS. Certain foods and substances, such as caffeinated drinks (soda, coffee, tea), can contribute to PMS. Many women have also discovered that when they are especially stressed, they experience worse PMS. The best way to understand it, and to figure out what might trigger PMS in yourself, is to pay very close attention to your body, your feelings, and your outlook. Many women have found that when they change their attitudes about their moontime, looking at it as a time of renewal rather than an annoyance or worse, their difficult PMS symptoms decrease or even disappear completely! It is often fulfilling to keep busy doing things you love to do, working and playing hard and being out in the world. But often our desire to keep going in the world keeps us from listening to our inner needs. PMS teaches women to balance *being* time and *doing* time.

REDEFINING PMS:
"PREPARING MYSELF TO SHINE"

Preparing: To make ready.

Myself: Me, the awesome person that I am.

Shine: To give out light, to be bright, to illuminate.

I used to have horrible PMS. I was grumpy and irritable, my skin broke out, I dropped things a lot, and I burst into tears at the simplest thing. It was as if all the emotions I had experienced during the weeks since my previous moontime, and all the worries I had carried with me, came bubbling up to the surface at the same time, about four days before the start of my period. I would try to ignore and push through the PMS, knowing that my body's discomfort and my distress would pass and I would feel better soon, but the cycle repeated monthly, and with each month a new symptom appeared — cramps, headaches, fatigue, and irritability.

Then I heard some women talk about the special ways they treated themselves just before and/or during their moontime. I was reminded of my friend Kali's note from her grandmother, Mama Maria, in which she reminded Kali to take special care of herself. I learned how to make new nutritional and exercise choices to help me through PMS, and I learned how important it is for girls and women to take time just for themselves.

I decided to give this stuff a try. As I mentioned, I knew that my symptoms were at their worst about four days before my period, so I chose that as my "day off from the world" day. No chores, no work; just time for me. I take walks, write in my journal, draw, and pamper myself with bubble baths, homemade facials, yummy food, and hanging out. During my period, I try not to push myself so hard. I lighten up and relax more. I daydream a lot. Having this one day (or, some months, a few hours or a half day) to myself completely changed my life and my moontime experience.

My uncomfortable PMS symptoms are almost no longer an issue and I feel great when my period arrives. My day off gives me time to feel rested, peaceful, and happy inside, so very soon, I am ready to go out and shine in the world once more. It just wasn't natural to expect myself to feel energetic and extroverted all the time. When I thought that way, I became frustrated and irritable with myself and other people. Now I love my downtime — time to just be quiet and introverted, time to enjoy my different moods. Downtime also stimulates and revitalizes my creativity. By the time I am ready to go back into the world, I am full of smart and creative new ideas, dreams, and visions. I feel balanced and inspired.

MOONTIME WISDOM

Every moontime cycle offers an opportunity to redefine yourself. Each month, you can take a little time-out from the world, be it a few hours or a day. You can use this time to let go of things that aren't working in your life, celebrate things that you like about yourself, pamper and nourish yourself and your beauty, dream a new dream, and come out ready for the world in front of you.

The greatest thing about a monthly time-out is that it

is in harmony with not only your body but also nature's own cycles. Nature has a built-in cycle of self-renewal that we can use to stay healthy, happy, and full of juicy good thoughts, energy, and inspiration. By observing the change of seasons, we see that in the winter, seeds lay in the darkness beneath Earth's surface, and once they are ready, they push up through the soil and grow beautiful flowers in the spring. In the summer sun they grow strong, and in the fall they die and their seeds return to the Earth to begin the cycle again. As with nature's changing seasons, each moontime cycle presents an opportunity to look within ourselves, grow quiet, listen, and emerge with renewed energy and vision.

A PMS TOOL KIT: GET TO KNOW, LOVE, AND DECIPHER YOUR MOODS

The days before moontime, when PMS usually occurs, are a perfect time to get to know more about yourself and your moods. Many girls and women find that this is a time when their feelings are easy to access because emotions are close to the surface. The following tools are part of my survival kit for moontime moods. I also added some ideas from other girls and women. Enjoy these tools, and create your own.

1. Create a moontime moods calendar. Each day, draw a picture that best represents your feelings on that day, and put it on that day's date on a calendar. After a few months, you might

notice a pattern starting to emerge: you might feel the same way on the same day of your cycle each month. You might notice similarities from month to month, or you might not. Try using the mood calendar for at least three months, and then see what similarities and patterns you notice. There are also apps you can use to track your periods and moods. If you have a cellphone or tablet, you can go to the App Store and search for "period tracker" to see many different ones to choose from. You can also use emojis to capture your daily moods' highs and lows.

2. Put your moods to work for you. Moontime can mean mood changes. And moods are the stuff that great art is made from. Draw your feelings; write down your most exaggerated and elaborate story about your dreams, worries, fears, and desires; or make beautiful art. Invite all your moods in. Get to know them. Then let them show you how to use them to bring your visions to life.

3. Remember that you are more than your emotions, even though some feelings can be very strong. They are here to show you something about yourself, but they are not you. You can feel them, and then you can let them go.

4. Remember the truth about feelings: no matter how you feel — happy, sad, mad, afraid, alone, confused, excited, frustrated, curious, jealous, spiteful — all feelings are okay, acceptable, and normal. How we relate to our feelings and what

we do with them is what matters. I felt so relieved when I learned this. I always had believed that if I had what I thought was a "bad feeling," something terrible would happen, or I thought that I was terrible for having that feeling. Then I learned that all people have pretty much the same feelings — it's what we do with those feelings that defines what our lives are like and how we feel about ourselves.

5. Find at least one person you can share your most real self and feelings with. This might be a friend, parent, teacher, counselor, coach, sister, or aunt. Or you can invite a group of your friends together and create a support circle. Support circles can include your friends or anyone else you really like and trust, like your mom or your aunt. You can meet and talk together, sharing your feelings and experiences. Support circles are great because you hear lots of people's ideas and feelings in a safe and caring place.

When I was a young girl, I thought I had to do everything alone. If I made a mistake, I was scared that I would disappoint people who mattered to me, so I wouldn't talk to them about it. If I was mad at those closest to me, I felt guilty, so I wouldn't say I was mad. I also thought I had to keep things secret. This was no way to live! Luckily, I had sisters and friends I could turn to, people who I knew would not judge me.

When I was eighteen, I learned about support

circles where I could share my feelings in a safe and accepting group environment. The more I learned to trust other people and to tell them what was going on with me, and the less I worried about being judged, the more I liked to share my feelings. I learned I didn't have to figure out my life all on my own.

Now I call my trusted friends almost daily with any concerns that I want to talk through and then be able to just let go of. I am amazed at how much sharing my thoughts and feelings with people I trust helps me to feel better inside and to make better choices in my life. You could invite your friends to join you in a support circle, a private group/friend chat, or weekly phone check-ins to share your feelings, experiences, dreams, and visions.

6. Help someone else. Sometimes this is one of the best ways to deal with stress. Offer a little service. Take care of a neighbor's garden, volunteer to help the Pad Project or another charitable organization, or help out at an animal shelter. When you do something to improve your community, you also improve your feelings about yourself.

7. When you feel sad, write in your journal, sing the blues, draw how you feel, take a walk, call a friend, hug a tree, or read poetry.

8. When you feel mad, give yourself permission to let all your anger out in a safe and creative way. You might feel like screaming into your pillow,

banging on a drum, kickboxing, punching a punching bag, or asking a friend if she or he will listen to you. Anger can be a powerful force, creating changes in our lives. It is destructive only when it is directed at ourselves or others in a hurtful way. You can express anger without harm in your journal, in song, in a dance, in sports, or in a play.

9. When you feel lonely, write a letter to yourself. Write everything that you long to hear from someone you love. Put it in an envelope, stamp it, and send it to yourself. Remember that even though you might feel lonely, you are never really alone. We are all connected by love — even if we can't always see it.

10. Support yourself by spending quality time alone — without your phone or computer. Just YOU time. If you have a good relationship with yourself, you will be able to handle anything that life brings your way. You will know how to follow your heart.

I learned about a saying that can help anybody in times of stress. It goes like this: HALT! And it's a reminder not to let yourself get too (H) hungry, (A) angry, (L) lonely, or (T) tired.

If you feel hungry, eat, even if it is just a little. This will keep your emotions steadier during your moontime. If you are angry, pause, take a breath, and call a friend to talk it out. If you are lonely, start a project that includes your favorite things in life — like making a scrapbook or decorating your bedroom wall. If you are tired, give yourself a break and take a nap. It is important, especially at your moontime, to support yourself by checking in on what you need.

 ## MOONTIME HERSTORY
Frida Kahlo

I never painted my dreams. I painted my own reality.

— **Frida Kahlo**

Frida Kahlo is known for her vibrant and fiery spirit and her love for and dedication to painting. Born in Mexico City to a Hungarian-Jewish father and a Catholic mother of Spanish and Native American descent, Kahlo survived polio to become a fearless and passionate young woman. In 1925, when she was eighteen, her whole life changed when she was almost killed in a bus accident that shattered her spine and pelvis. Defying a prognosis that she wouldn't survive or walk again, Kahlo used her recovery time — and her emotional and physical pain — to begin to paint. Her art was also influenced by her great love affair with Diego Rivera, another gifted artist. She is an amazing example of a woman who made art from a painful experience, and who created a passionate and beautiful life. During PMS or other times when you experience strong feelings, you can put all those feelings into creating something beautiful, like Frida did. Feelings are the main ingredient in art.

PMS AND NUTRITION

Good nutrition is a very important part of caring for yourself. It can make a big difference in the way you look and feel, especially in relation to your period and PMS.

Here are some easy and helpful things to remember. The week prior to your period, make an effort to reduce your intake of salt, sugar, red meat, soda, and caffeine. This will help your blood flow easily, lessen any bloating, and help your skin look radiant, too. Eat whole grains and plenty of fresh fruit and vegetables. If you do these things, you will notice how good your body feels.

Some women notice that warm food and drinks are most nourishing and comforting during their moontime and help to prevent cramping.

It is important to get plenty of vitamins and minerals, especially calcium, to help yourself develop a healthy and strong body. It's best to eat a variety of foods, especially leafy greens and foods rich in calcium, which include yogurt, soy milk, calcium-fortified orange juice, cheese, tofu, and broccoli.

The following is a sample menu of foods that are good to eat during PMS. To find out what is best for you, try writing down all your favorite foods. Then see which ones make you feel best during moontime — you can decide to leave those foods on your moontime menu and take others off. Taking enough time to enjoy yourself and appreciate your food while eating is important, too.

MOONTIME MUNCHIES
A Moontime Menu

I like to eat comfort food during my moontime, and warm comfort food can soothe the pain if you experience cramping. Here are a few of my favorite moontime recipes.

Cramp-Relief Raspberry Tea

Raspberry tea is known for its healing properties and has been used for centuries for women's menstrual health.

To make a cup or a pot of delicious steaming raspberry tea, use 1 tea bag or 1 tablespoon of loose tea leaves for each cup. Add steaming-hot water and let the tea steep for a few minutes. If you like, you can add a bit of honey and a crescent moon–shaped orange wedge.

Super Sassy Soup

If you are going to feel moody during your moontime, you might as well feel sassy! While preparing Super Sassy Soup, get in touch with your sassy self by thinking of different things you can add — maybe bell peppers or potatoes or other spices. Try out different variations of this recipe and adjust it to your perfect liking. Preparation time is about 40 minutes.

Serves 6 to 8

Ingredients

  2 tablespoons coconut oil
  1 large onion, chopped
  2 bunches carrots (about 2 pounds), peeled and sliced
  1 stalk celery, sliced
  2 teaspoons salt
  4 medium cloves garlic, minced
  2 teaspoons ground cumin
  2 cans unsweetened coconut milk
  4 cups chicken or vegetable broth
  Freshly ground black pepper to taste

Heat the coconut oil over medium heat in a soup pot. Add the onion and sauté until the onion is starting to look clear.

Reduce the heat to low and add the carrots, celery, salt, garlic, and cumin. Sauté for 10 minutes, stirring occasionally. Add the coconut milk and broth and bring to a boil. Stir, cover, and let simmer 30 minutes. Season with pepper and serve. Yum!

Mystical Muffins

There is nothing better than the smell of freshly baked corn muffins wafting through the house when all I want to do is wrap myself up in a blanket and lie on the couch with a great book and a cup of raspberry tea. These muffins take about 10 minutes to prepare and 15 to 20 minutes to bake. You will need a muffin pan.

Makes 12 muffins

Ingredients

1½ cups unbleached white flour

½ teaspoon baking soda

2 teaspoons baking powder

½ teaspoon salt

1 cup yellow cornmeal

1½ cups milk

1 egg

5 tablespoons melted butter

4 tablespoons dark molasses

3 tablespoons sugar

Dash of cinnamon

Preheat the oven to 375 degrees. Lightly grease 12 muffin cups with butter, unless they're nonstick.

In a medium bowl, sift together the flour, baking soda, baking powder, and salt. Stir in the cornmeal, then make a well in the center of the dry ingredients.

In a separate bowl, using a spoon or whisk, beat together the milk, egg, butter, molasses, sugar, and cinnamon. Pour this mixture into the well of the dry ingredients, and stir just enough to combine thoroughly.

Fill the muffin cups just up to their edges. Bake for 15 to 20 minutes or until a toothpick inserted all the way into the center of a muffin comes out clean.

Remove the muffins from the pan right away and cool on a rack for at least 10 minutes before eating. Enjoy with a pat of butter, with your soup or your tea, or just as is. Scrumptious!

THE ART OF PAMPERING

Pampering and delighting in your gorgeous self is one of the best things about being a woman. Caring for your skin, especially during times of body changes, is also important. You might like to make a whole day or night of it. Indulge by yourself or invite a friend to join you for a pampering party.

 ### MOONTIME MAGIC

PMS Pampering: A Do-It-Yourself Fun Facial in Three Easy Steps

To prevent breakouts, try these facial treatments. They are easy to prepare, feel great, and smell delicious! All your senses will be delighted, and your skin will glow and tingle.

Fresh Fruit Facial Cleanser

Ingredients
    3 ripe strawberries
    1 ripe peach, peeled and pitted
    2 teaspoons rose water (found at your local
        health-food store) or chamomile tea
    1 tablespoon face cream (any gentle moisturizer
        or cleanser suited for your skin type)

In a medium bowl, crush the strawberries and peeled peach together. Strain the juice (you can drink it, discard it, or mix it in a yummy smoothie). Stir the rose water or chamomile tea and the face cream into the crushed fruit, and mix all ingredients together. Apply the mixture liberally all over your face. Let it do its magic for 5 minutes, then rinse thoroughly with warm water. For best results, follow with the Miracle Mask (see below).

Miracle Mask

Ingredients

- 1 egg white
- 1 teaspoon honey
- 3 or 4 drops lavender essential oil

In a small bowl, mix all the ingredients together. Apply the mask to your face, avoiding the eye and upper lip areas. Lie back (this will keep the mask from dripping down your face) and relax for 20 minutes, or until the mask is dry. You could use this time to try the PMS Remedy meditation below. Rinse off with warm water. Follow with Cooling Cucumber Toner (see below) and moisturizer. This feels great and makes the skin radiant.

Cooling Cucumber Toner

Ingredients

- ½ cucumber, unpeeled
- 3 teaspoons witch hazel
- 1 teaspoon mineral water or lavender water

Place the cucumber in a blender and puree it. Using a spoon, stir in the witch hazel and water, then strain the liquid through a sieve into a bowl or jar. You can discard the pulp. Dip a cotton ball in the liquid mixture and dab it on your face. Refrigerate the leftover liquid. (Any recipes with fresh fruit or vegetables must be used within three days.) Follow with your favorite moisturizer. Notice how your skin tingles and glows!

MOONTIME MEDITATION
PMS Remedy

Find a place to sit or lie down and relax. Close your eyes. Take a few deep breaths.

Notice how your body feels. Where is it relaxed? What does that feel like? Where is it tense or uncomfortable? What does that feel like?

Let your breath travel to the tense places. As you breathe in, let the breath gently relieve the tension. Imagine any worries or fears leaving your body with your exhalations. As you inhale, imagine breathing in warm golden light. Allow the warm light to travel through your whole body, especially to any cramped or blocked areas.

See the light dissolving any blocks, allowing energy to move freely through your body. See and feel your body relaxed, healthy, and vibrant. When you feel that this meditation is complete, open your eyes.

MOONTIME JOURNALING

"Preparing Myself to Shine"

Take out your moontime journal. Write about what your perfect self-care day would include. Consider your list a reminder to treat yourself with gentleness each month. Here is a sample list of simple things you can do:

Stay in bed longer
Take walks
Eat delicious, healthy food
Paint your nails
Write poetry
Daydream
Give yourself a facial

Read a book
Take a bubble bath
Meditate
Play music
Paint, draw, doodle…
Just be

If you indulge in self-care and pampering during your moontime, you will find yourself looking forward to your cycle each month, and you will truly redefine PMS as *preparing myself to shine*!

MOONTIME MOMENTS

Luscious Bubble Bath

Treat yourself to a magical moontime bath! Add twelve drops of your favorite essential oils and bubble bath gel to the tub under running water. Turn off the lights and (with permission) light a candle. Luxuriate in your bubble bath while letting your mind wander.

Chapter Four

BEING A GIRL, BECOMING A WOMAN

It's a long, long road. It's a big, big world.
We are wise, wise women. We are giggling girls.

— **Ani DiFranco,** "If He Tries Anything"

WHAT IT MEANS TO BE A GIRL

Have you ever thought about what it means to be a girl? Or about how to define being a girl? I think that we can define being a girl by how we each experience our "girl-ness." Our definition can also include how the world defines a girl. It is a constantly changing definition, and the more we learn to positively define ourselves through our own experiences, words, beauty, strength, intelligence, and infinite creativity, the more we will influence the way the world at large defines girls. The roles and meanings of girls and girlhood have changed many times over thousands of years — and they can also depend very much upon the time and culture a girl lives in.

To me, being a girl and becoming a woman mean that I am blessed with the power and magic of creativity and that I am connected to nature. Having a female body means that I have a menstrual cycle, and that cycle connects me in a very physical way to nature's larger cycles. Nature's cycles are perfectly balanced. This means that if I carefully pay attention to the natural rhythms and cycles of my body, the dreams in my heart, and the ideas in my head, I can do anything I dream of doing, because I have a built-in natural system of balance and support. My definition of being a girl (and now a woman) is that I am fun, creative, strong, assertive, shy, silly, beautiful, interesting, powerful, feminine, tough, smart, energetic, outgoing, reserved, and everything in between. I am myself. Being a woman means I am free to be full of contradictions and to embrace the individuality that makes me me. Being a woman means that I am love, grace, and beauty in motion. I am magical and amazing. I am connected to all life. I have the power to create.

Many things can influence your definition of a girl, and your definition of yourself as a girl. The way you think of yourself and what you learn from your family, friends, school and community, country, the media, and history all shape your definition. I have found that defining what it means to be a woman for myself is important because it gives me the power to influence how the world defines me. I won't settle for any external definition of myself — I define myself first, and I continue to redefine myself as I grow and change throughout my life. Self-definition is important for every girl and woman.

How do you do this? I first acknowledge my female body and its rhythms; then my personal interests, talents, and desires; and then my personal history, my ancestral history, and women's history. Acknowledging all these aspects of myself gives me the opportunity to shape and dream my own future because I know that I carry many experiences within myself. This knowledge gives me strength and carries me forward. I like finding role models, too, among girls and women I admire. This helps me to expand my views and my beliefs and to imagine the possibilities of what it means to be a girl or a woman.

 ## MOONTIME MYTHOLOGY

The Great Mother Goddess's Blessing

This passage is from the book *Flowering Woman: Moontime for Kory*, by Shinan Barclay and Mary Dillon.

> "The Great Mother Goddess has blessed women," whispered Chalice, the Grand Mother of the West. "She has given us our moontime. Our moontime is for renewal, for nourishing our inner strength, for getting in touch with our deepest feelings and for expressing our power. This special time is to re-attune to our own personal rhythm so we can begin our cycle again pure and strong. It is the

time when the Goddess is most likely to use each woman as a channel to pour out her truth and beauty in the form of songs, poems, stories, new ideas and new ideals. Guard this special time of your moon. Don't make yourself so busy that you have no time to do the work of the Goddess. Because she brings a special blessing for us all."

WHAT GIRLS SAY ABOUT BEING A GIRL

The following are quotations from girls about what it means to them to be a girl or a female.

Being female means something different for everyone, and there is no right or wrong way to self-identify as female.

— **Willa Bennett,** Seventeen.com

Being a girl means finding power in my voice and the validity of my own experience and story. It can be hard to navigate through pressures of family, classmates, and society, but I feel a certain gratitude for and comfort in the sisterhood of other girls and women who encourage me to keep going and to take up space in this world!

— **Mimi,** 16

Being a girl means I can be anything I want. When my grandmother was my age, girls did not think they could have any career they wanted. I am glad it's not like that anymore.

— **Mary,** 12

I think being a girl means that I have to be responsible, because someday I might be a mom, and I want a good place for my kids to have fun.

— **Madeline,** 13

Being a girl means being everything: strong and soft, smart and kind, compassionate and pragmatic, spontaneous and responsible, sympathetic and unabashed. The challenge is learning to accept what I am in any given moment, knowing it is always changing and not needing to apologize for it.

— **Kaela,** 17

My mom likes being a girl because she likes to have fun in everything she does — she says girls know all the secrets to having fun in life.

— **Cristina,** 14

Being a girl means not being afraid of standing alone. It is during your moments of independence that you can develop self-respect and self-esteem.

— **Alisa Harvey,** professional runner and NCAA running champion

MOONTIME MEDITATION

Seeing Yourself Grow from Birth to a Young Woman and Beyond

This is a really cool meditation. Lots of girls like to have their journals close by for this meditation so they can write about their experiences afterward. Keep a pen handy, too. Remember, you can find this and the other meditations in this book at www.yourmoontimemagic.com!

Take a few moments to get comfortable, lie down, and relax. Take three or four deep breaths all the way into your belly, letting your body relax more and more with each exhalation.

Imagine yourself as a newborn infant, just birthed from your mother's womb. See your tiny hands and feet, your little nose and eyes and lips. Notice the small, rapid breaths that move your chest up and down. See how perfectly formed you are, how innocent and in need of love and care. See how you easily drink in food and nourishment. Imagine all the love in the world flowing into this baby girl.

When you are ready, see how, with love and care, this baby girl begins to grow from an infant into a toddler. See her body grow, her teeth, her hair. See how she smiles at the sun on her face or at a gentle breeze as she plays outside. Watch her begin to walk with the support of her parent's hand. See all the love in the world flowing toward her.

Now see this toddler as she turns into a young child, growing still more, getting taller and stronger. Imagine her as she learns to talk, to read and write, to play sports, to draw, and to do all the things you like to do. See how she enjoys feeding herself well, taking naps, playing hard, learning new things, and just being. See how she giggles with her friends. Once again, imagine all the love in the world flowing toward her.

Envision this young child becoming a more independent girl. Notice how she feels in her taller, stronger body. See what she loves to do and how she likes to play. Imagine all the love in the world flowing toward her.

Now see this young girl growing older still. Notice that her body is beginning to change shape.

Place your hands on your belly. Take a few minutes to notice your own body now. Think about your life today. See yourself with your friends, and think about what makes you happy. See yourself nourishing your body with healthy, good food. Imagine moving your body in play, sports, or dance. Notice how you feel in your body. Think about what interests you most in the world. What are your dreams? How does it feel to be you today? Now feel all the love in the world flow into your own body. Your body becomes warm from head to toe, surrounded with love and support.

Finally, look into the future, a few years from now. See how your body has changed and grown even more. See how comfortable you are in your body; notice the smile on your face. See how your future self loves her life.

Imagine all the love in the world flowing toward her. In your imagination, ask your future self if she has any advice that might help you as you grow during the next few years. Listen gently to what she says.

When you are ready, ease your attention back to today. Open your eyes and come out of the meditation. You might want to stay centered and write about your experience. Or you might want to share it with someone. Pay attention to the lessons you taught yourself, and honor the feelings you experienced.

MOONTIME JOURNALING
Thoughts about Girls

Find a place to hang out, and take out your moontime journal. Complete the following sentences:

Being a girl means…
What I like most about being a girl is…
The hardest part about being a girl is…
My mom thinks girls are…
My dad thinks girls are…
Images of girls I see on videos or social media make me think that being a girl means…
I think girls are…
A girl I really admire is _____, because she…
A woman I really admire is _____, because she…

MOONTIME MAGIC
Butterfly Transformation

Draw a picture of a butterfly. Growing from a caterpillar into a winged creature, the butterfly is nature's expert on the art of transformation! Pretend your butterfly is carrying your worries away and representing the exquisite woman you are becoming.

As you grow from a girl into a woman, think about the kind of woman you aspire to be. Choose role models who display qualities you admire. You can ask yourself how you think your role model might handle a certain situation that you are dealing with. If you aspire to be a great athlete, perhaps you think of Simone Biles or Serena or Venus Williams. If you aspire to be an activist, perhaps you think of Malala Yousafzai, Emma González, or Greta Thunberg. If you aspire to go into politics, perhaps it is Alexandria Ocasio-Cortez. Role models help broaden our definition of ourselves and fill our lives with possibility.

Remember to define yourself on your terms first and that as you do, you will influence a positive definition for other girls and women in the world.

Chapter Five

BODY CHANGES

Like the seed within the flower,
like the flower within the seed,
the hidden things will be revealed,
if you believe, if you believe.

— **Kelli Love,** "Semillas"

Your body changes every moment of every day. We are always in transition, whether we notice it or not. We experience transitions many times each day — the day turns to night and then to day again, we move from our home life to our school life, from friend time to family time. We experience transitions over the years, too, as we move from being children to teenagers to adults. Change is a constant in our lives. It is reflected in the seasons, too. Sometimes it feels great, and sometimes it feels awful. Accepting that life is full of transformations, and learning about specific changes, helps you to find creative ways to be a part of all this change, rather than feeling that change just happens to you.

Enjoying and getting to know your changing body are important because the body is powerful, amazing, and capable of so many incredible things. As you are already aware, your body's changes might be different from those of other girls' and women's bodies. But we all undergo most of the changes I describe below.

Your skin will go through a change as you turn from a girl into a woman: It might be oilier or prone to breakouts sometimes. Or it might get drier. The main change you will notice is that your skin will need just a little more care than it did when you were younger.

Your breasts will develop and grow fuller, and you will need to wear comfortable underclothes — bras and sports bras — for support. Your hips might widen. Your body will grow hair in new places — on your pubic (genital) area and under your arms. The hair on your legs might grow and become darker. All these changes are normal, expected, and part of growing up.

When I first noticed my body changing, I was about eleven years old. My best friend and I talked about body changes a lot. One night she slept over, and she told me she was starting to "get hair down there." We both screamed and laughed. I felt excited about my body changing, but kind of nervous, too. When I was twelve, my breasts began to develop, and my mom bought me a bra. In those days, it was called a training bra. (I know: lame name!)

Some of my friends were already much more developed

than I was. I wasn't sure how I felt about that. I wanted to stay a kid, with my kid's body, and not worry about bras and periods and what my body looked like compared to my friends'. I was also excited about my body changing, and I liked dressing up in my older sisters' clothes. I liked looking in the mirror and imagining how I might look in a few more years.

But it was those in-between years that were the hardest. I felt like I had no control over anything happening to my body. I was growing taller but not wider, so I was super-scrawny, with bony knees. My skin started getting pimples. My feet were too big for the rest of me, and I was very clumsy for a while. I tried to make up for that by getting a new hairstyle. I wanted that long, wavy, pretty hair that some of the actresses I saw on TV had. I ended up getting a really bad perm that frizzed my straight blond hair. Then I had to get braces as well. I felt very awkward. Mostly, I wanted to find a cocoon to hide in until this whole transformation thing had happened. I wanted a lot of privacy and would feel incredibly self-conscious and exposed at the slightest comment about me or my appearance.

The hardest part was that I thought other people saw me in the horrible and awkward way I was starting to see myself — and the truth is, they didn't at all. At this point, I think, I mentally separated myself from the changes in my body because they seemed way too uncomfortable. I just tried to ignore the changes that were happening or to pretend I didn't notice them.

Another uncomfortable change was the new attention

my friends and I received from other people. My very embarrassing aunt exclaimed in front of the whole family, "Oh, you are starting to blossom! Look at those breasts!" I really wanted to shrink away. I noticed how the boys in my school paid a lot of attention to the more developed girls, and I wondered if I would ever develop as they had. It was all just so unknown. And I dreaded the occasional gross stares from older men on the street. It seemed that so many changes were taking place at once. Some were great, but many just upset me.

By the age of fifteen, most of the changes had happened, and believe it or not, I loved my new body. I loved the way my clothes fit my new curves and how strong my growing body felt. But there were some rough times. The most helpful thing I did was talk to my friends about those times, and I realized that we were all in this growing-up thing together. Sharing our nightmare moments, like my aunt's totally weird comment, made us laugh for hours. Really, I don't think there is anything better than laughing with friends about all the oddness we experience as our bodies shift and we try to catch up with them.

"My Changing Body" by Lizzy, 16

It's one of those things that just makes you want to close your eyes and wake up when it's all over. At first it's like, "Dear God, please help me out of this awkward stage! Let me open my eyes and be a woman!" But after a while — I can't explain it — I suddenly took a deep breath and realized it's not that bad. It's like you blink and suddenly you are comfortable in your own skin, excited and almost breathless at the inner workings of your own body. I could let go of my sadness at feeling like a door had closed, and realize that maybe new doors were opening. I am part of all women, connected by Mother Earth's cycle. To me, my period is magical now; I feel blessed to be in this body, so blessed to have been a girl and so excited to become a woman.

A FIRST-MOON CELEBRATION STORY

Laura's parents are from Israel and have been living in the United States for the past thirteen years. This year, they were concerned about Laura because she was diagnosed with spinal scoliosis and had to have surgery to help correct it. Spinal scoliosis creates a curve in the spine that can become worse over time. The surgeons fused parts of her spine together and inserted metal rods and screws in her back to keep it straight. The whole ordeal lasted several months and included many days of painful recovery and physical therapy. Laura lost ten pounds, which her parents feared would delay her first moon. They knew not only that the onset of menstruation would welcome Laura into her womanhood but also that the hormonal changes in her body would slow down the scoliosis's growth.

Now Laura is in eighth grade and has just had her first moon. Laura's entire family celebrated. Her mother, father, and brother danced and called their relatives in Israel with the news so that they, too, could join the celebration. This summer, Laura and her mom will take a trip to France together to celebrate her arrival into womanhood.

MOONTIME MYTHOLOGY
Rosh Chodesh

Women and the moon have long been linked in many traditions and religions. Rosh Chodesh, the Jewish new moon festival, is traditionally recognized as a women's holiday. A marker of the new month (the Hebrew calendar is based on the moon), Rosh Chodesh is God's reward to women.

GROWING-UP ADVICE FOR GIRLS, FROM GIRLS AND WOMEN 15 TO 50

- Grow into and get to know your new and changing body through dance or sports.
- Be in your body.
- Give yourself all the privacy you want to create a cocoon, and while you're in it pay more attention to your inner self or write or paint about what you are going through.
- Be a witness to your own growth.
- Touch and view your body; get to know it!
- Write poetry.
- Hang out with fun, supportive girls. Host a girls' circle and support one another.
- Go out for team sports.
- Journal.

- Learn about all the cool changes your body is going through.
- Remember that even though some girls don't show it, all of us go through this passage, and it ain't always easy!
- Talk about your changes and feelings with your mom or a trusted older woman friend.
- You are the only you here. Only you can bring the gifts of who you are to the world.
- Stay true and honest, and you can handle anything!
- Sometimes the bad stuff turns out to be good.
- You are enough just as you are!
- Remember, all those girls on Instagram or YouTube most likely are using filters and are airbrushed. They're not real!
- It can be fun to wear revealing clothes and to celebrate your body. But, unfortunately, we live in a world where not all people feel the same way. Be aware that what you wear attracts attention, and some of it you might not want. Choose your clothes with care and awareness so that you always honor yourself!
- Surround yourself with people who respect you and treat you well.
- Your body is beautiful, strong, and healthy. Each body has its own cycle, rhythm, size, and shape. Each body is a beautiful work of art.

Who run the world? Girls!

— **Beyoncé**, "Run the World (Girls)"

BODIES IN MOTION

Being happy and comfortable in your body and with its changes has a lot to do with how your body feels.

Does your body feel strong and healthy to you? Do you feel fit? Exercise is an important part of caring for your changing body. It also helps to promote a healthy menstrual cycle and reduces PMS symptoms, including cramping. What do you like to do for exercise? Take walks? Dance? Play sports? Everybody is different, and some types of exercise might be a better fit for you than others. For example, my daughter Chloe loves aerial yoga. My goddaughter Lizzy loves long-distance running but cannot stand being in a gym. My niece Fran loves to hike and rock climb. Mary loves yoga. Kaela adores spin classes. Jen loves to walk. Kelli dances hip-hop for hours. Finding out what you love to do and making it a part of your life are among the best things you can do for your body and your health.

Exercise releases natural chemicals called *endorphins* in your body that actually make you feel good. I love running long distances. I don't like running really fast, but I do like slow, long runs on mountain trails. They give me time to be out in nature and to unwind from all the events of my day. Out on the trails, it is just me and the sound of my feet carrying me on the path. Sometimes I talk out loud to the trees — or the flowers and rocks — around me; sometimes I just talk in my head. I like to have conversations with nature about everything going on in my life and to ask for answers or solutions to problems I am having. By the end of my run, my head is always clear and answers are easy to find.

I've discovered another good thing about running (and other individual sports): every time I make it through a long run, it adds to my confidence in my ability to make it or come through in other areas of my life. Whenever I feel a crisis of confidence, I go for a run. Feeling the strength of my muscles and the way my body can move across the land reminds me that I am strong — inside and out — and that I can handle whatever challenges face me. Running not only makes my body even stronger, it also builds the strength of my mind and confidence.

Keeping It Balanced

Whatever you do for exercise, remember to listen to your body and to do what feels good. When it is time to play, play. When it is time to rest, let yourself rest. It's important to keep your nutrition, exercise, and rest time in balance.

Sometimes athletes, especially those with a very low body-fat percentage, such as gymnasts or long-distance runners (who have to put in hours of workout daily and adhere to a strict eating plan), may have late puberty or may stop getting their period. This is called *female athletic syndrome* (FAS). Once a young woman cuts back on exercising and gains some body fat, her period will resume. However, prolonged FAS can lead to bone damage and other problems like osteoporosis (weak bones) later in life. If you miss your period more than three times and if your weight is low, check in with your doctor.

MOONTIME MEDITATION
Thanking Your Body

Find a comfortable place to sit or lie down and relax. Take a few deep breaths, and let yourself relax more with each exhalation. See your body in your mind's eye, and take a little time to check in on it.

Place attention on each area of your body, starting with your head. Let your hands move to each area and rest there as you say "hi" to it.

As you see and feel your head, thank it for all the thinking it does each day. Thank your hair for its warmth and for the way it feels when a breeze blows it against your skin. Thank your eyes for showing you the beauty of the world. Thank your ears for the music they let you hear. Thank your nose for introducing you to the sweet scents of flowers. Thank your mouth for letting you enjoy delicious foods. Thank your throat for singing and speaking.

Now thank your arms for hugging. Thank your hands for touching. Thank your heart for loving. Thank your skin for feeling the warmth of the sun as well as the chill of the wind. Thank your belly for being your center, for balancing you as you move in the world. Thank your womb for bleeding, for connecting you to the greater cycles of life. Thank your legs for walking and letting you stand. Thank your feet for taking you where you want to go.

Now take a few moments to breathe into your whole body, and thank your breath for breathing life into you each moment. When you are ready, open your eyes, enjoying your body and your senses and the gifts they are.

MOONTIME JOURNALING
Body Gratitude

Take out your moontime journal. Write about how you felt during this moontime meditation. What do you like about your body? What gifts does your body give you?

MOONTIME MAGIC
Create Your Own Magical Mist

Flower essences and essential oils are wonderful healing gifts from the Earth. Flower essences are extracts that carry the energetic imprint, or personality, of the flower but have no scent. Essential oils, which are used in aromatherapy, are oils extracted from flowers or other parts of plants, and each one carries a unique scent that promotes physical, emotional, and spiritual health. Every flower essence and essential oil has its own personality; no two are alike. Flowers are amazing healers.

Flower essences and essential oils work wonderfully together. You can combine them to use in your bath or as a pillow spray. You can use them for help with fears and moods, for creative inspiration, for healing, to ease physical pain, and for skin and body care. It's fun to create your own mixtures and to create them as gifts for friends.

You can purchase flower essences, essential oils, and spray bottles at health-food stores or order them online. Before you buy, it's a good idea to decide which flower essences you want by reading about them in books or online. Remember that flower essences have no scent, so you will select them based on their special healing gifts. Take a trip to your local health-food store or specialty shop and give yourself time to sample the scents of various essential oils. Be sure to ask the retail professionals any and all questions you might have about the products they are selling. Once you have decided on a couple you like, you might want to read about which healing qualities these oils have. Trust yourself on the ones you want to use. There is no "right way" to choose an essential oil for yourself. Just have fun and pick out what you like.

Have fun trying out new scents and essences. When you have created your own misting spray based on the recipe below, you can spray it directly on yourself or around your room, or use it on your pillow at night to give yourself sweet dreams.

Magical Moontime Mist

This mist of essential oils and flower essences might be helpful for you around your moontime. It smells and feels divine, and it is my all-time favorite.

Rose oil is calming and emotionally healing. It can also be worn as perfume. Roman chamomile oil is calming and helps to balance emotions. Pomegranate flower essence promotes a healthy attitude toward the start of menstruation and balances the forces of creativity. Alpine lily essence helps to promote a healthy relationship with menstruation and body development. It also helps to harmonize your feelings about your female body with the emotions and feelings in your heart. Chamomile flower essence helps with mood swings and balances emotions.

Supplies

- Small spray bottle, empty and clean (I like the pretty blue glass ones often sold in health-food stores or online)
- Stickers, ribbon, and/or metallic pen(s) (optional)
- 4 ounces filtered, spring, or purified water
- 6 drops rose essential oil
- 3 drops Roman chamomile essential oil
- 2 drops pomegranate flower essence
- 2 drops alpine lily flower essence
- 2 drops chamomile flower essence

Before you begin, it can be fun to decorate your bottle with stickers, ribbons, metallic ink, or any other wonderful touches.

Take the cap off the spray bottle and pour in the water. Place the drops of each essential oil and flower essence into the water. Replace the cap, shake well, and mist the air around your face.

 ## MOONTIME MOMENTS
You Are Beautiful

Look in the mirror and say to yourself, "I am beautiful, and I love my body!" Do this every time you see your reflection. Seeing your own beauty helps to keep it alive. See the beauty of others, too — your ability to do so is a reflection of the beauty within you.

Chapter Six

BODY WISDOM

You are beautiful, no matter what they say.
Words can't bring you down, oh no.
You are beautiful, in every single way.
Yes, words can't bring you down, oh no.
So don't you bring me down today.

— **Christina Aguilera**, "Beautiful"

Your body has great wisdom; let it show that wisdom to you! When treated with care, your body is your greatest friend. It can tell you everything you need to know.

 MOONTIME HERSTORY

Moontime and the Origins of Healing

Some of the most ancient human artifacts ever discovered are about thirty-seven thousand years old. They are small statues of female humans who were believed to be the guardians of the Earth. The statues were used to remind people of the mysterious power of the female to create and care for life on Earth.

Since the beginning of time, women have been great healers, and they have learned to heal by listening to and caring for their bodies. Early observation of the menstrual/lunar cycle helped women develop healing skills. Observation of this cycle also helped people develop time measurements, numbers, and calendars!

Learning to take care of your body is a central part of women's wisdom and can lead to all kinds of wonderful discoveries.

TRUSTING YOUR BODY WISDOM

Listening to and accepting your body and the messages it sends you is the surest path to a healthy, beautiful body. By becoming quiet and listening to yourself, you can quite easily discover how to best care for yourself. Health is the natural harmony and balance that arise within the body and spirit when they are properly cared for, and all it requires is your willingness to listen. Some days, perfect health might mean eating a lot and resting. Other days, perfect health might mean exercising and laughing a lot.

BODY WISDOM AND INTUITION

Besides telling you all you need to know about how to take care of your physical needs, listening to your body also gives you all the information you need to take care of yourself in any situation. This skill is called *intuition*. I like to think of my intuition as the part of myself that is always awake and paying attention, even if I am sleeping or distracted. My intuition is my own personal antenna.

The more you pay attention to the messages your intuition sends you, the sharper or more finely tuned your antenna becomes. For example, when some people are in an unsafe situation, they experience intuition as a queasy feeling in their stomach that tells them it's time to leave. Intuition is the part of themselves that tells them that, even though everything might look okay on the outside, something isn't right about a person or a situation.

Your intuition can clue you in as to whether someone is being honest with you. It can also guide you to try out a new class or sport by giving you a little nudge from within, a little excitement at the idea of trying something new. And intuition can even help you be "lucky": sometimes, when something that seems lucky happens — for example, you're in the right place at the right time — you can look back and remember little messages or feelings you experienced that urged you to be there. That's intuition, and it is invaluable. It is your own personal bodyguard and dream maker. It is your personal healer and friend. If you learn to listen to your body and give yourself time for quiet, you will be able to develop a very strong understanding of your intuition and how it works. And by following your intuition, you will always be able to make good choices for yourself.

Trust yourself! Listen to your body and its desire for hugs, movement, dance, play, and sports. Take time to just chill. Hang out, sit, stretch, walk, read, and cry if you need to. The body is the physical expression of the spirit, so by doing what your body wants you to do, you can come to know your spirit. As you grow and express your beautiful self in ways that you love, your body grows stronger and healthier, and your spirit shines more and more.

MOONTIME MOMENTS
Body Art

Celebrate your body with body art. You might like to experiment with henna tattoos or body paints. They are colorful, temporary, and perfectly safe. Maybe you will want to paint a moon and star on your ankle or a butterfly on your wrist.

MOONTIME MEDITATION
Listening to Your Body

Find a comfortable place to relax, lying down or sitting in a chair. Let your eyes close, and take a few deep breaths.

Tighten all the muscles in your body as much as you can, then release them all and exhale. Do this again. Notice how your body feels resting on the ground or in the chair. Are you comfortable? Do you need to adjust yourself to find a better position? If so, do that now. Feel your breath rising and falling in your chest. See the breath travel through your body, nourishing all your cells, massaging and relaxing your muscles.

Using your mind's eye, scan through your body. Are there any tight or tense areas? If so, bring your attention there and focus your breath into these areas. Take several breaths until the tightness has released.

When you are relaxed, ask yourself, "What does my body need from me today?" Placing your hands on your belly and breathing in, listen for your body's response.

When you feel that your meditation is complete, begin to wiggle your toes and come out of your meditation, ready to respond to your body's needs.

 ## MOONTIME JOURNALING
Body Reflections

Take out your moontime journal. Write about your meditation. How did/does your body feel? Were you able to release any tightness through your breath? What messages did your body have for you today? Write them down. What can you do today to respond to your body's needs and be your own healer? Write down your plans.

 ## MOONTIME MOMENTS
Moontime Massage

Massage is a great way to prevent and relieve pain, balance emotions, and help you feel healthy. *Acupressure* is a type of massage that places pressure on certain points on the body, called *acupressure points*, to assist in healing. Acupressure points are special points that correspond to the various muscles and organs and to your energy. It is perfectly safe to use acupressure on yourself or someone else. Just pay attention to what feels good so that you don't press too hard, which *won't* feel good! Here are three acupressure massage techniques to try, the first for menstrual pain, the second for balancing the emotions of PMS, and the third for an excellent massage at any point during your moontime.

Massage for Menstrual Pain

Several acupressure points are important for this massage. Points 1 and 2 are on the back at waist level, in the muscle bands beside the spine. The rest of the points are on the front of the body. Point 3 is on the stomach, directly below the navel and in line with it. Points 4 and 5 are on the lower edges of the hip bones. The last pair, points 6 and 7 are on the lower legs: on the inner shins beside the shinbones. (Don't press these points on a pregnant person, as that can bring on bleeding.)

A good beginning is simply to rest your hand on the general area of one of these points while you take a deep, relaxed breath. Then, using your fingertip, press gently on the point. Move your finger around the area, continuing to press gently until you feel a slight dip that tells you that you've reached the exact point. Press it lightly, holding the point until you feel the tissue underneath your fingertip soften and relax. Then slowly press into the point. It may be sensitive or tender to the touch.

By pressing into a point in this way, you unblock it so

that the body's energy can run freely through it (which relieves any discomfort). When this happens, you will feel a slight pulsing or throbbing, like a heartbeat, under your fingertip. Recognizing this pulsing takes some practice, but soon you'll start to notice it easily. Hold each point for about 30 seconds.

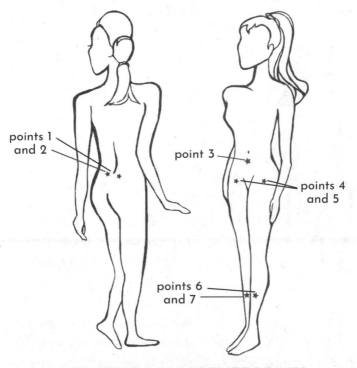

points 1 and 2

point 3

points 4 and 5

points 6 and 7

MENSTRUAL PAIN RELIEF POINTS

PMS Massage for Emotional Relief

The first pair for this massage, points 8 and 9 are under the collarbones, where they meet the shoulder joints. Massage with small circular motions until you feel your body relax. Another good spot is on the little-finger side of each wrist, in the hollow of the wrist joint; these are points 10 and 11. Again, gently massage each spot with small circular motions. As you do so, you can play sweet music and think nice thoughts for yourself.

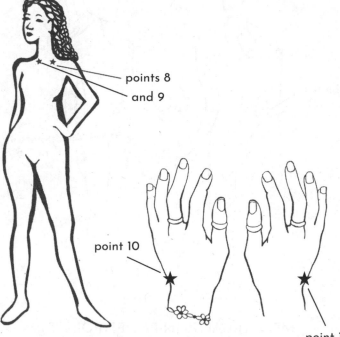

points 8 and 9

point 10

point 11

PMS RELIEF POINTS

Moontime Monthly Massage

For an easy do-it-yourself massage that feels wonderful, rub six drops of essential oil with massage oil onto your lower abdomen. Continue rubbing in a circular clockwise motion for several minutes to ease pressure and relieve cramping. Then let yourself drift off to a dreamy sleep.

Massage with Friends

You can do massage with your friends. Use massage oil and take turns giving one another foot massages. There are acupressure points above the heel and just below the anklebone, and rubbing these can be very soothing at moontime.

For centuries, women's healing and body wisdom came from observing a woman's menstrual cycle. Paying attention to your own cycle, and what makes you feel good, will support you to be in good health throughout your life. Listening to your body's needs and responding will also strengthen your intuition. Following your intuition will help you be healthy, safe, and confident.

Chapter Seven

BODY IMAGE

How Your Self-Image Helps to Create Your World

I'm not the average girl from your video, and I ain't built like a supermodel, but I learned to love myself unconditionally because I am a queen.

— **India Arie**, "Video"

I love my body. I love how strong and healthy it is and how it carries me through my life. I love my eyes. They are big and blue and can see forever. I like my hair. It is blond and shiny, and I can wear it up or down, straight or curly. I like the way it feels on my skin in a breeze. I think I have a very special nose: sometimes I think it is unique and kind of Romanesque; other times I think it is pointy, like a fairy-tale witch's. But my nose lets me enjoy the amazing scents of roses and jasmine in the garden and of fresh bread baking in the oven. I like my lips and my mouth, for with them I can kiss and I can talk. I like my shape, the curves of my breasts and hips. I like my belly button. I like being ticklish. I love the feeling of wrapping myself up in a warm towel when I'm fresh out of the shower, and resting in that clean, warm, skin-tingling sensation. Bodies are amazing.

When I was eleven, I didn't like my body very much. I didn't like my forehead, my knees, my wrists, or my nose. I wanted to hide all these parts of myself all the time. One day, my friend commented that I had a big forehead, and from that day onward I always wore bangs. Even when I swam, I was so self-conscious about my forehead that I would pull my wet hair down to hide it, which made everyone laugh.

A few years later, another friend said, "You would be so pretty if only you got a nose job!" After that, I became totally obsessed with getting a nose job. I even visited a plastic surgeon to discuss it. He greatly discouraged me and said that I had a "delicate nose" that was in fact unique and Romanesque and that he thought it perfectly suited the rest of my face.

I spent many years trying to become like a girl in a magazine. I truly believed that if my nose were smaller or my body thinner or if I had better skin, I would be really great and have a perfect life, and everyone would love me. While trying so hard to be the image of perfection that I saw in all the magazines, I lost many chances to enjoy myself, my friends, school, and work. I lost out on learning to listen to and appreciate my body. Trying to make myself into some outer idea of beauty or perfection left me feeling pretty hopeless and somewhat empty.

I think my "aha" moment came when I learned that

all girls, no matter what they look like, have similar fears and worries about themselves. Most girls also spend more time and money than they want to on trying to look like the images in magazines and on social media, which girls imagine they should resemble. But in fact, even these girls have the same worries and fears!

I noticed that the girls who seemed happiest to me were the ones who were really into something they loved. Observing them, I decided to try something different. I decided to keep enjoying the fun stuff about beauty — like dressing in clothes that I loved and that made me feel good and taking good care of myself by eating right and exercising. But I also decided to lose the worry and negative self-talk. I decided to focus my energy on things that I really liked and was interested in — like training for a marathon, reading books (fiction and nonfiction) about women I loved and admired, writing, acting, and learning about the environment. Doing these things was what really changed my self-image and made me happy. Through this process, I learned that I have no control over how the world views me — no matter how "perfect" (or not) I look. I also learned that I needed to start being a lot nicer to myself. I cannot depend on the world to be nice, and I cannot depend on what the world defines as "beauty," but I can define beauty for myself — and that makes an impression on the world around me.

And by the way, these days my hairdresser is always trying to get me to grow out my bangs and push them off my face. She says I have the most beautiful forehead, and she doesn't want me to hide it. I'm still thinking about that one!

MOONTIME HERSTORY
Misty Copeland

It's about the journey and enjoying and loving the body you're in now and enjoying the process of getting to wherever you want to go.

— **Misty Copeland,** speaking to students
at Harvard University

Misty Copeland is a ballet dancer for the American Ballet Theatre (ABT). She did not start ballet lessons until she was thirteen years old, at a local Boys & Girls Club, and by seventeen she was a professional! In 2015, Copeland became the first-ever African American woman to be promoted to principal dancer in the ABT's eighty-one-year history.

Misty faced discrimination and other challenges daily on her way to this great success. "It took me a long time to understand and dissect the words that a lot of minority and black dancers in particular, hear," such as "You don't belong in the classical ballet world because your feet are too flat. Your butt is too big," she said. "I see dancers who are professionals who have these bodies who are white. Why am I being told my breasts are too big? Why am I being told my body is too muscular? It's code language for your skin is wrong."

Today, Misty supports other girls and women to love their bodies, to nourish them with healthy foods, to meditate, and to go for their dreams!

MOONTIME MEDITATION

The Girl in the Mirror

Find a comfortable place where you can sit in front of a mirror by yourself. Using a brush, comb, hair pick, or your hands, comb through your hair. If you don't have any hair, or have shaved your head, use your hands and gently rub and appreciate your scalp. Some mystics believed that a woman's hair (or scalp) is her transmitter to the world — and to her spirit. As you comb through your hair or rub your scalp, notice how beautiful it is. If you have any thoughts about it that you don't like, put them aside for now and just focus on appreciating your hair: the way it keeps your head warm on cold days, the way it blows in the wind, or how nice it is to braid and decorate with ribbons, bows, and barrettes. Feel how good it is to gently comb it. If you are focusing on your scalp, notice how soft it is, how good the warmth of the sun feels on your skin, how fun it can be to decorate it with scarves or body paint or soft hats.

Take a minute to look at the reflection of your eyes. Notice the small specks of light that bounce off your irises. Notice all their colors. Look at and touch your face — your eyes, nose, mouth, and skin. Think about how your nose lets you enjoy a fragrant day in spring. How your skin tingles on a cold morning or glows in the sunshine. Notice how your mouth lets you communicate when you need to, lets you say beautiful, kind things and express yourself. It lets you sing and share ideas, eat nutritious food, say surprising and shocking things. Your words can change the world!

Take a few minutes to really enjoy your reflection. Look at yourself and say, "I am beautiful" three times. Say it again until you can feel it without any doubts all the way into your belly.

You can take it up a notch: turn on some music and dance and sing in front of the mirror. Be a rock star or hip-hop dancer. Have a blast. Make up your own song about why you are the best thing to ever happen to this world. You are beautiful — through and through.

Remember, you are more than your face. You are more than your body. You are a beautiful, precious, wonderful young woman inside and out, and you are very loved!

MOONTIME JOURNALING
Finding Your Own Beauty Moments

A Journal Entry by Kelli, 12

Who am I?

I am beautiful because I give so much of myself to the world.

I am powerful because my spirit is strong and unconquerable.

I am great because I am committed to living my dream.

I am strong enough to endure the challenges of life.

I am really good at listening with an open mind and heart.

I really love to sing, climb trees, be barefoot and naked, laugh, and play.

I think my eyes are round, deep, and starry. They show my true feelings and my soul. I like my eyes because my sight is precious and my vision is honest and open and beautiful.

I think my ears are curly, small, and a delicate pink like a pig's tail. They are very sensitive. I like my ears because they feel good and allow me to hear.

I think my mouth is expressive and my lips are big. I have a beautiful voice that sails on the wind. I like my mouth because it allows me to communicate, to sing, to kiss, to laugh, and to eat.

Now, take out your moontime journal and complete the following sentences:

My mind is…
I like my mind because…
My hair is…
I like my hair because…
My eyes are…
I like my eyes because…
My nose is…
I like my nose because…
My ears are…
I like my ears because…
My mouth is…
I like my mouth because…
My hands are…
I like my hands because…

My arms are...
    I like my arms because...
My heart is...
    I like my heart because...
My breasts are...
    I like my breasts because...
My stomach is...
    I like my stomach because...
My hips are...
    I like my hips because...
My butt is...
    I like my butt because...
My vagina is...
    I like my vagina because...
My legs are...
    I like my legs because...
My feet are...
    I like my feet because...
My body is...
    I like my body because...
My moontime is...
    I like my moontime because...

WORKING TO END PERIOD STIGMA AND PERIOD POVERTY

Nadya Okamoto is committed to making a difference for girls and women living in period poverty. Nadya experienced homelessness during her teenage years, and she found that one of the many struggles homeless girls and women face is access to period products. To address this need, in 2014, when she was sixteen, Nadya started the nonprofit PERIOD with her friend Vincent Forand. Based in Oregon, it now has over 450 campus chapters in all 50 US states and in over 30 countries. It has become the largest youth-run nonprofit for women's health, fighting period poverty and period stigma through education and advocacy! It provides women access to the period products that they need and empowers girls and women to feel confident and clean every time they have their period. To learn more about Nadya Okamoto, you can watch her TEDx Talk and other inspiring videos on You-Tube (go to YouTube and search for "The Menstrual Movement") or visit the PERIOD website (www.period.org), where you can also click on "Get Involved" to find out about volunteering or starting your own chapter.

 ## MOONTIME MOMENTS
Inner Spring Cleaning

Sometimes, when I am not feeling great about my outsides, it means that I have been looking at too much social media filled with pictures of airbrushed models or with filters, and comparing myself to them (argh!), or that I am not thinking many good thoughts about myself. That means I need to do some "inner spring cleaning."

Take out a sheet of paper or your moontime journal

and title it "What I Can't Stand about Things Right Now." Then list every single thing that is bothering you, anything that upsets you, everything that is bugging you. For example, maybe you hate all the clothes in your closet, or you hate that your friend scored higher than you on a test at school (and she didn't even study!), or you are mad that the person you have a crush on at school isn't paying attention to you, and on top of all that you can't stand the president! Whatever it is, write it down. It is a huge relief to get it all out and not carry it around with you.

After writing the list, you might feel that's all you want to do. Or you could look it over and see if there is any one thing on the list that you could do something about — any situation that you could improve, anything that you could do that might make you feel better about it. For example, if you hate the clothes in your closet, you could take them all out, invite friends over with the clothes they no longer want, and have a clothing swap. Or you could sell them at your local consignment shop and use the money to build a new wardrobe. Taking action works like magic to help you feel better about yourself and your life. You have the power to make a change!

Sometimes, making changes on the inside by doing a little inner spring cleaning makes us want to do the same on the outside. Maybe it's time for a new haircut or style. Enjoy trying out new images of yourself. Experiment and have fun.

Chapter Eight

DREAMS

The Power of Moontime Dreaming

The future belongs to those
who believe in their dreams.

— **Eleanor Roosevelt**

D reams are magical and surprising. They are doors we can travel through to reach whole new worlds. There are so many different kinds of dreams: daydreams, night dreams, lucid dreams, visions, and premonitions, to name only a few. Some women find that their dreams are more vivid or that they can remember them more easily at certain times of their cycle. Some women dream more while they are ovulating; others dream more during PMS; and still others dream more while they are menstruating.

When you dream, there are no limits. Everything is possible. In your dreams, awake or asleep, you might be an eagle soaring above the trees or a mermaid swimming in the deep blue ocean. In your dreams, you are completely free.

Native Americans believed that when a woman is menstruating, the veil between this world and the next is very thin and that it is now easier for her to dream and make contact with other dimensions. They believed that a woman's dreams during her moontime could tell the future of the tribe, and so the tribe treated her dreams and moontime as sacred.

 ## MOONTIME MYTHOLOGY
The Wisdom of Isis

In ancient Egypt, Isis was revered as a powerful goddess, a protector of children. Her mythology tells of how the evil god Seth cut Isis's husband, Osiris, into pieces that he scattered all over the land. Isis found and gathered the pieces of Osiris, magically restoring him to life.

The story of Isis reminds us that even when we feel our lives are falling apart, within us is the magic we need to restore ourselves and rebuild our lives.

In ancient times, people who honored the Goddess Isis would go to one of her temples to sleep and dream. Sleep restores our bodies and minds, and dreams can restore our emotions. Inside Isis's temples were mirrors. The mirrors were a reminder of the importance of self-reflection. In her temple, her worshippers tended their inner lives and reflected on the messages of their dreams.

The wisdom of Isis teaches us to pay attention to our dreams. They offer us insight every night, and by reflecting on them, we can be restored.

DREAMING DEFINED

Dreaming occurs in many different ways. The following are some general descriptions of various types of dreams.

Daydreams: Daydreaming is the experience of letting your thoughts drift off and your imagination wander while you are awake. This could happen while you're sitting through a boring class or lying on the grass watching the clouds drift by.

Night dreams: Every night as you sleep, your body enters different stages of sleep and dreaming. REM, or rapid eye movement, is an important sleep stage and is the time when most of your dreams happen. REM sleep allows your mind to let go of or dump all the events of the day, so that you can wake up refreshed and ready to take on a new day.

Nightmares: As you probably know from experience, nightmares are frightening dreams. Some common nightmares include being chased by someone but being able to run away only in slow motion, or trying to scream but not being able to make a sound. Nightmares can be your mind's way of working out fears you have in your life. For example, when my niece was a child, she dreamed that she was being eaten by a whale. Her best friend at school had a very overpowering personality and was physically stronger than she was. As she learned, with the help of both of their moms, how to say no to her friend when she felt overwhelmed, this nightmare went away.

Lucid dreaming: Lucid dreaming occurs when you are asleep and dreaming and realize that you are dreaming and that you can influence the dream. For example, I had a recurring dream of being chased by a man. Then a friend told me that the next time I had the dream, I should confront the man and say, "Stop it." I wasn't sure how I could do this while sleeping, but I did. The next time I had the dream, I felt as if I woke up inside it and said to myself, "Oh, yeah, I am having this dream again. Now I can turn around and tell him to stop." As I ran, I turned around, looked at the man, and said, "Stop chasing me!" At that moment, I grew into a giant woman and the man looked really small, the size of an ant. It was a great feeling.

When I journaled about it later, I wrote that I thought the man represented all the little daily things that I worried I couldn't handle. But when I took a minute to deal with them directly, I realized that they are little concerns — nothing that I can't handle!

Learning that I have control in my dreams and my nightmares has helped me with many challenges in my waking life.

Visioning: Visioning is when you have a clear thought or feeling about something that hasn't happened yet. This experience is sometimes also called a *premonition*. You also vision when you consciously imagine something that you would like to come true. This is often called *visualization*, and it can be a tool for defining your goals and reaching them or for facing your fears and overcoming them. For example, you might envision yourself feeling completely relaxed and confident while speaking in front of your class, or hitting a home run for your team, or even waltzing down the halls of your school on the first day of your period, feeling completely carefree about cramps or stains. Visioning simply means purposely imagining something you would like to see happen in reality. You'll learn more about it in chapter 9.

MOONTIME HERSTORY
The Gifts of Dreams

My dreams have always been interesting to me. I love trying to figure out their meanings and work with their messages. Sometimes the messages or gifts from my dreams are really clear to me, and other times they are much harder to figure out, but they are always valuable in some way. In fact, this book is the result of a dream I had. One night I dreamed that a "Great Mother" or goddess figure said to me all the things that I wish I had heard when I had my first moon and went through adolescence.

It was a beautiful dream. When I woke up, I wrote down everything she had said. That was the start of this book! I visualized moms giving it to their daughters as a gift to celebrate their moontime. I visualized how it might be for young women to hear about celebrations from all over the world and about how incredibly special, beautiful, and celebrated they are.

I wrote the original draft, added illustrations, and sent it off to publishers. I also gave homemade copies to my nieces as gifts to celebrate their first moon. I loved how happy they were to receive it. Every week for several months, I visualized my book being published and imagined how I would feel when it was complete.

Initially, the book didn't find a publisher. I was disappointed, but I still kept my sample copy on my dresser, put a wish in my Goddess Box (see an explanation of Goddess Boxes in chapter 12), and went on with my life and other creative projects. Three years later, when I was least expecting it, a publisher called. She said she had received the book years earlier and loved it. So you are now reading the result of that sweet dream I had years ago. Getting to know your dreams and what they mean can take you on wonderful and unexpected journeys.

Create a beautiful space for sweet dreams. Surround your bed with pictures and items that make you feel good. Then let your dreams take your imagination, ideas, and goals to new heights.

HOW TO REMEMBER YOUR DREAMS

Sometimes it can be hard to remember your dreams. Here are a couple of things you can do to make remembering them easy.

- Take a small glass of water to bed. Just before you lie down to sleep, drink half of the water while saying to yourself, "When I drink the other half, I will remember my dreams." Upon waking, drink the other half, and you will remember your dreams. You might need to try this a few times to "train" your mind, but eventually it will work.

• Keep a dream journal, or use your moontime journal, to record special dreams you want to remember. Once you get into the habit of recording your dreams, you will find that it becomes easier and easier to recall them.

UNDERSTANDING WHAT
YOUR DREAMS TELL YOU

Dreams often reflect themes — ongoing events and feelings — in your life. There are many common "dream themes," things that lots of people dream about. For example, many people dream of huge tidal waves. This can mean that a big change is coming or that strong feelings are rising to the surface. During transition times, this dream and dreams of earthquakes are common.

Learning to understand your dreams is a fun way to learn more about yourself. This is great, because the more you get to know and understand all the parts of yourself, the more comfortable and happier you will be and the easier it will be for you to understand other people. Purchasing a dream dictionary or checking one out from the library is a good idea. You can also seek out online dream dictionaries. In them, you can look up other common dream themes, like sleeping through the alarm on the day of a test at school, being naked in front of the class, falling, or flying.

MOONTIME MEDITATION
Bringing Your Dreams to Life

This might sound too simple to be true, but it really works. First, find a comfortable place to sit or lie down and relax. Take a few deep breaths. With each inhalation, imagine breathing in love and happiness. With each exhalation, imagine any worries or stresses leaving your body. Continue this for several breaths.

Now, resting quietly, think about something you would like to bring to life. For example, is there anything you really dream about doing? Publishing a book or a blog article, working on something important in your community or the environment, recording a song? Whatever it is, let yourself ask for help on how best to achieve your heart's desire. Rest here and listen quietly for a response. It might come in the form of your voice in your head giving you advice, or as an image of a person you realize you could call on for support, or as some other symbol. Or the answer could come to you in a dream while you are sleeping. Once you have asked for help, trust that the answers and support will come. Just listen and look for the response.

When you are ready, bring your attention back to the present moment, stretch your body, blink your eyes, smile, and know your dreams are on their way to coming true!

MOONTIME MYTHOLOGY

A Lakota Story of the Dreamcatcher Legend

Lakota wisdom tells us that long ago, when the world was young, an old man sat on a high mountain and had a vision. In his vision, Iktomi, the great trickster and teacher of wisdom, appeared in the form of a spider. Iktomi spoke to him in a sacred language that only the old man could understand.

As he spoke, Iktomi the spider took the elder's willow hoop, which had feathers, horsehair, beads, and offerings on it, and began to spin a web. He spoke to the elder about the cycles of life, about how we begin our lives as infants and move on to childhood and then adulthood. Finally, we reach old age, when we must be taken care of as we were as infants, completing the cycle.

Iktomi said, "In each time of life there are many forces that can help or interfere with the harmony of nature, and also with the Great Spirit and all his wonderful teachings." Iktomi gave the web to the Lakota elder and said, "See, the web is a perfect circle, but there is a hole in the center of the circle. If you believe in the Great Spirit, the web will catch your good dreams and ideas, and the bad ones will go through the hole. Use the web to help yourself and your people to reach your goals and to make good use of your people's ideas, dreams, and visions."

The elder passed his vision on to his people. Even today, many people use the dreamcatcher as the web of their lives. It hangs above the bed or elsewhere in the home to sift dreams and visions. The good parts of our dreams are captured in the web of life, but any bad dreams escape through the center hole.

 ## MOONTIME MAGIC

Make a Dreamcatcher

You can make your own dreamcatcher, or, better yet, invite a few friends over and make them together. Search for a dreamcatcher tutorial on YouTube — there are many of them. When you find one you like, gather the supplies you'll need, follow along with the video to create your unique dreamcatcher, and then hang it above your bed to catch your most expansive dreams!

Dreams bring you on many wonderful journeys. In dreams, you are completely free. You can fly, jump over tall buildings, and travel to other worlds. As mentioned earlier, many women notice that their dreams are more powerful and vivid at different times during their menstrual cycle. Sometimes dreams carry special messages and gifts for you. As you learn to pay attention and listen to your dreams, many magical things can unfold. Sweet dreams!

Chapter Nine

VISIONING & VISUALIZING

Bringing Your Dreams to Life

i bleed
every month.
but
do not die.
how am i
not
magic.

— Nayyirah Waheed

Your dreams and visions are your gifts to the world. By living them, you bring happiness and healing to others and give them permission to live their own dreams. By living your dreams and visions, large and small, you make the world a better place.

 ## MOONTIME HERSTORY
Ellen Ochoa

In 1993, Ellen Ochoa traveled on the space shuttle *Discovery*, making her the first-ever Hispanic female astronaut.

In January 2013, she made history again by becoming the first Hispanic and second female director of NASA's Johnson Space Center. She reflected in an interview, "I can only imagine the amazement and pride my grandparents would feel, having been born in Mexico in the 1870s and knowing that their granddaughter grew up to travel in space." Thanks to their move to the United States to raise their family, along with the examples set by her mother, who put herself through college as an adult, and Sally Ride, the first American woman astronaut, Ellen dared to envision herself in outer space and take the steps to get there. She said, "I encourage all Latinas and women to seek out interesting, challenging careers." Embrace your dreams, for your flights of fancy might turn into flights of much greater dimension.

WHAT IS VISIONING?

As mentioned in chapter 8, visioning is the act of imagining and focusing on something your heart desires; it is a way to help bring that thing to life. Visioning, or visualizing, can help in every area of your life. Visioning clears the way for dreams to come true. Visioning helps you easily remove any barriers to achieving your goal, such as fears or other kinds of resistance. Visioning can be helpful for school, sports, relationships, and health, as well as for other things, such as becoming a rock star or working for world peace.

Visioning requires only that you set aside time each

day (or week or even month) to be grateful for something (or many things) in your life today, and to think about exactly what you want. As you imagine what you want, fill in all the details: what it looks like, how it makes you feel. Leave the question of how it will actually happen for your spirit to figure out. While visioning, all you have to do is to imagine your dream as you really want it to be. Start carrying it around in your heart and thinking about it daily, believing it is possible. Every time you think of it, reassure yourself that this dream is coming to you. And absolutely believe that if it doesn't come, that is because something *much better is on its way to you.*

Our job as visionaries (people who vision) is to do our best to live healthy lives by caring for our minds and bodies and by enjoying ourselves completely and treating ourselves like the amazingly beautiful and magnificent queens that we are. We must each have the courage to dream big dreams, to vision them regularly, and to take steps to bring our dreams to life. The most important thing is that visioning is fun and brings you happiness. When you feel that, know you are on the right track.

Women are creators. Each new thought we think, each new dream we dream, can be brought to life if we follow our natural cycle. The moontime cycle is like our bodies' own waterfall, washing away and cleansing that which we no longer need, connecting us to the Earth, making room for our visions, and bringing them to life. Fill your mind with beautiful music, art, and poetry. Create a fertile ground for your dreams to grow in!

Examples of Visioning and How to Do It

Have you ever heard the expression "Worrying is like praying for something you don't want to happen"? I love that saying. Our thoughts have a lot of influence on the rest of our lives. If we think good thoughts, especially about ourselves, chances are that we will have happy lives. If we think negative thoughts or worry much of the time, chances are that we will limit our happiness.

I like to visualize what I want instead of worrying about what I don't want. I do this for myself, for my friends and family, and for the world. Visualizing during your moontime can be especially nurturing, creative, and fun. Moontime is a natural time for reflection and quiet, and visioning is a very relaxing and sweet experience. Visioning during our moontime can do the groundwork for the rest of the month, so that when we are ready to take up our busy lives again, everything will unfold with grace.

Visioning and Parents

Visioning about issues you have with your parent(s) can be very helpful and sometimes kind of magical. For example, if you and your parent(s) have been stuck in an argument that you don't know how to resolve, try visioning. When you have some time alone, close your eyes and relax. Let all your worries and frustration about this situation go. See yourself letting them go. Put them in a big red helium balloon and watch it float high into the sky, up and away. Good!

Now imagine yourself sitting with your parent(s) in whatever place you usually talk together. Imagine that each of you is filled with love and support. Let yourself sit in these warm feelings. Imagine you can see the flow of love between you and your parent(s). Know that each of you wants to reach the best possible solution. In your meditation, tell your parent(s) what you want them to hear. Share all your feelings with them. Then tell them you trust that their decision will come from love only, because you know that you are loved no matter what. Now listen to see if they respond to you in your meditation. They might or might not.

When you bring your attention back to the present moment, try to also bring back all the good feelings of love and support. The next time you talk to your parent(s) about the issue, notice if anything changes. You might be pleasantly surprised! Generally, when people try this, they may not always get the exact outcome they wanted, but they usually have a much happier one.

Visioning and Friends

If you are having trouble with a friend — for example, maybe you don't get along as well as you used to, or maybe she did something to hurt your feelings — try visioning.

As in the above example of visioning with your parent(s), first imagine that you and your friend are surrounded by love and support. Relax into that feeling. In your visualization, see yourself speaking freely and with care to your friend. Let her know what is on your mind and in your heart. As you speak to her directly, remember and trust that this can work out. Now listen for her response. Notice what you feel in your body. Do you feel relieved, more relaxed, and happy?

Or maybe your friend is having a rough time and has shared with you that she is struggling with her parent(s) or another friend. After you have supported her by listening, you can visualize good things for her. Instead of worrying, you can visualize her surrounded with love, support, and good feelings. You can see her laughing and having a very happy day. You can do this each morning for a week as a gift to her. Visualizing good things for the people we love feels really great.

It can also be powerful to vision *with* your friends. Sometimes, especially when I have a big-time vision to consider, I like to take turns visioning with a friend. We each share our vision and then vision each other's dream together. This usually takes about five minutes per vision. When we finish, we talk about what we saw for each other and for ourselves in our vision. It is so much fun, and it's especially exciting when we both experience or see the same thing.

Visioning for Health

Did you know that some hospitals now use medical intuitives to help patients heal and recover from surgery? *Medical intuitive* is another term for a healer — someone who might use "integrative" techniques for healing, such as visioning, massage, and other types of treatments. Medical intuitives are sometimes invited into the surgery room. During surgery, their job is to focus on or imagine the patient as completely healthy and whole and the surgery as going perfectly. Whether the technique is proven or not, patients treated by intuitives often feel so much better compared to those who aren't that doctors are starting to see the real value of visioning, both for oneself and for others.

Use visioning to imagine a perfectly healthy body or to heal from a wound or injury. Imagine the injury completely healed and well. Imagine any cramping from your moontime going away, and see all the muscles in your body relaxed and healthy. Visualize clear and radiant skin.

Visioning for School and Sports

Visioning can help you improve your performance in many areas of your busy life. For example, you can use it to help you write a challenging paper or report. Imagine easily finding all the information you need to write the paper. See yourself having fun, enjoying the writing process, and turning in the paper on time. Imagine the completed paper and how you feel when you're finished. See the smile on your face.

You can vision for other purposes, such as preparing for a speech or performance. Use the same process. In your meditation, see yourself on the day of your presentation. See yourself surrounded by love and support. See how happy you look, feel how confident you are, and feel that confidence in your body. See how natural your performance is and that you easily remember everything. Imagine completing the performance and your relaxed and satisfied feeling. See people smiling around you.

You can definitely use visioning to alleviate any worries you have about getting your period at school. Visualize yourself playing sports, walking happily down the school hall, or at the school dance feeling great and totally confident in your tampon's or pad's ability to prevent leaking.

Visioning is also perfect for sports. Some professional teams vision together while preparing for a big game. And top athletes use virtual reality (used in this way, technology can enhance visioning) to experience themselves making the plays or moves to succeed. If you have a competition coming up, you can use visioning to see yourself easily making it over the hurdles in the track meet or to see your soccer team "in the zone," working together to bring yourselves a victory.

MOONTIME JOURNALING
The Desire List

It's time to tell yourself what you want — *everything* that you want! Take out your moontime journal. Across the top of a blank page, write "My Desire List" and today's date. Next, write down the first thing you can think of that you want; write it as a complete sentence beginning with "I want." Below that, affirm your desire by writing a sentence, in the present tense, as though you already have that thing (see the examples on the next page). Continue in this way until you've listed every single thing you want in your life, followed by an affirmation sentence.

Hang a copy of your list on your mirror or another

place where you can easily refer to it. Look at it often. Each time you get something you desire, check it off your list, feel your gratitude, and write a new one. This is very satisfying and helps you to believe that following your heart's desire makes your dreams come true.

Examples of desires and accompanying affirmations:

I want to change the stigma around periods.
> *My period is natural and normal!*

I want some new earrings.
> *I have beautiful new earrings that I love.*

I want more time to hang out with my friends.
> *I have so many fun times with my friends.*

I want to take singing lessons.
> *I love my new singing lessons.*

I want to travel to faraway lands.
> *I love traveling in India, Australia, and Brazil.*

I want to feel happy in my body.
> *I love the way my body looks and feels.*

I want to accept myself just the way I am.
> *I accept and love all of me.*

I want to get along better with my brother.
> *My brother and I are finding better ways to communicate.*

I want healing for my aunt who is sick.
> *My aunt is healed.*

I want to be included with my friends and to include others.
> *I include others in all I do, and my friends include me.*

I want peace and healing at all borders.

   There is now peace and healing at the borders.

I want the whole world working together to stop climate change and help heal the Earth.

   Together, we are healing the planet.

I want the homeless people I see to have sunshine and shelter so they won't have to sleep under benches to protect themselves from the cold rain.

   Everyone has shelter.

I want people to be accepted for who they are.

   I accept myself the way I am today.

If you want to take this exercise one step further, write down your visions or goals for next week, next month, next summer. Then write three things you can do that will help you reach each goal.

Always ask for everything you want — you just might get it. Ask — even if you are scared to ask for what you want or think that it might be too much. Just by asking, you let other people help you figure out ways to get it!

MOONTIME MOMENTS

Making Your Room a Place for Your Dreams to Come True

For centuries, the ancient Chinese art of feng shui has been used to promote harmony and balance in every area of life: wealth, relationships, family, romance, health, creativity, and travel. During your moontime, and when you're thinking about your visions, you might like to create a special place where you can just rest and recharge. Feng shui can help you do this.

Your bedroom is probably the perfect place. Decorating and setting up your bedroom to attract all the good stuff you want in your life can help your dreams come true. It's easy to "map" your bedroom according to feng shui principles. Here's how:

1. First, take time to clear out any clutter in your room. Go through your closet and dresser and put anything you no longer want in a "give-away" pile. Clean out your desk and your backpack, too. I like to use an exercise from Marie Kondo, bestselling author of *The Life-Changing Magic of Tidying Up*: Pick up an item and ask, "Does this spark joy?" If it doesn't, thank it and put it in a give-away pile. Kind of like Ariana Grande's song, "Thank U, Next."

   Next, imagine that your room is divided into nine sections, each one associated with a particular area of life, as shown in the diagram on the next page. The wall that has the main doorway to your room would be the bottom border of the diagram, below "Knowledge," "Career," and "Helpful People and Travel."

   Your layout should look like this:

Wealth	Fame and Reputation	Relationships and Romance
Family and Health	Tao	Creativity
Knowledge	Career or School Goals	Helpful People and Travel

2. Decorate each of the nine regions of your room with items related to the corresponding subject area shown in the diagram. Of course, depending on the shape and setup of your room and how much furniture you have, this might not always be possible (for example, the "Tao" section in the center might be taken up by your bed, or the "Family and Health" section might be occupied by a bathroom door), but do what you can. (And if you're tempted to rearrange furniture, be sure to get a parent's permission first.) Here are objects that will work best in each area of your room, helping you to attract more of what you need:

- **Knowledge:** Bookcase with how-to books on your favorite subjects. I keep books by authors that inspire me most.
- **Career or school goals:** Mirrors or water-related items; images that support your career goals. Hang pictures on your wall of women in the career field that you aspire to; if you want to be a doctor, hang a picture of a woman doctor.
- **Helpful people and travel:** Pictures of people who help you in life and artwork or cultural items from places you want to visit.
- **Family and health:** Family snapshots, photo collages, and plants.
- **Tao:** You! Your own energy and intuition, and the coming together of energies from every area of your room.
- **Creativity:** Musical instruments, art supplies, artwork, and/or your computer. I keep a box of crayons and pictures of my kids playing at the beach. It is even a place for pictures of your pets!
- **Wealth:** Money, jewelry, fish, or fountains; anything red, purple, or gold. This is a fun area to decorate. I have a ceramic bowl filled with foil-covered chocolate coins.
- **Fame and reputation:** This area represents how others perceive you in the world. Candles, awards, or plants, as well as anything red, orange, or purple, are all good suggestions. I

have a framed list of qualities that I aspire to, such as "strong, fair, honest, creative," in this area of my room.

- **Relationships and romance:** Round or oval mirrors, anything pink, pictures of loved ones, paired objects (like two candlesticks or two crystals). I keep a pink orchid in this corner, a written note reminding me to express kindness and understanding to myself and others, a picture of me with my boyfriend, and two matching candlesticks.

Make your room as beautiful as you want, so that every time you walk into it, you feel like a very special goddess coming into your private palace, the place where your dreams are born.

 ## MOONTIME MEDITATION
Think Good Thoughts

Find a comfortable place to sit or lie down, preferably on the ground outside. Take a few deep breaths. Let your body relax with each exhalation.

Picture a beautiful crystal-blue waterfall at the top of your head. Imagine the lovely water pouring into your head, washing through your entire body, and pouring out into a stream that runs into the ground. Let it wash away any thoughts that you no longer need, any problems that are stressing you out, and anything that is bringing you down.

Now fill your mind's eye with a clear vision of what you want for yourself. For example, imagine the kind of day you would like to have, the kind of presentation you want to make at school, the part you'd like in the school play, or the after-school job that you've been hoping for. Make your vision as clear as possible, seeing all parts of the picture.

Now check in with your body. Imagine how your body will feel when this vision becomes reality.

VISIONING TO BRING YOUR DREAMS TO LIFE

After I have visioned, I usually experience a lot of synchronicity. *Synchronicity* is the experience of being in the right place at the right time, or thinking about something you desire and suddenly seeing or hearing things related to your desire everywhere you go and with everyone you talk to. For example, when I was visioning about this book, over the course of several weeks I met several women who did some kind of work with teenage girls, and some worked on the topic of menstruation. It's funny the way life works. Visioning is a way to invite into your life all the people and situations that will help bring your dreams into reality.

 ## MOONTIME MAGIC
Make a Vision Map

Vision mapping is another way to envision your dreams. It's especially fun to do with friends.

Supplies
   Magazines
   Scissors
   Large piece of posterboard or cardboard
   Glue and/or tape

Once you've gathered your supplies, close your eyes and let your mind wander to your biggest dreams. Think of everything you want and dream of, and also think about the little everyday things you love.

When you are finished visualizing, open the magazines, and, for the next twenty minutes, cut out any pictures, images, or words that remind you of the things you love, what is important to you, and, most of all, your biggest, wildest dreams. Glue the pictures and words onto the posterboard in any way you choose.

When you're done, share your vision map with a friend. Hang it on your wall, where you can see it each day, and watch as your dreams come true.

Chapter Ten

FRIENDSHIPS & CONNECTIONS

How They Change as You Grow

A FIRST-MOON CELEBRATION STORY

Lisa was born in Iraq and lived there until she moved to the United States at sixteen. When Lisa was ten, she had her first moon. In her family, this was cause for great celebration — it marked Lisa's entrance into womanhood. Her mother let all her women relatives know that Lisa's first moon had arrived. Her grandmother adorned her in gold bracelets and necklaces. Faraway relatives sent gifts of gold. They celebrated Lisa's rite of passage throughout that entire year. Her grandmother told her that when she was menstruating, she should indulge herself with good things and treat herself extra-special. She felt very loved and respected.

When Lisa was sixteen and moved to America, she noticed that women didn't celebrate their periods in the same way and that they did not think as highly of their periods as she and her family in Iraq did.

Lisa, now in her early forties, never experienced PMS or cramps. It is thought that girls and women who treat themselves with care and celebrate their periods have much less PMS and cramping. Now Lisa's own daughter is eight. When she has her first moon, Lisa plans to make it special for her daughter, just as it was for her. She hopes that every month, she and her daughter will have a "mother-daughter" day to celebrate their womanhood and their connection and to do something relaxing and perfectly indulgent, just for the two of them — maybe go get their nails done, maybe take a walk by the ocean. She hopes her daughter will like that, too.

MOONTIME MYTHOLOGY
The Moon Lodge

Historically, in many cultures, women went to a *moon lodge*, or *menstrual hut*, together during menstruation. This was a monthly time for women to be together, tell stories, and care for themselves. In the hut or lodge were young women who had just begun their menses, women of childbearing age, and women close to the end of the menstruating years. They were all together for a few days each month.

In the moon lodge, women told stories about how to best care for their bodies, about coming of age, about their relationships, about childbirth, and about all the many experiences they had as women. Young girls were able to get an up-close view of what to expect. They were able to see changes occurring in the women's lives around them and to learn how to take care of themselves. By learning to trust their bodies' cycles and to allow feelings to emerge within themselves, young girls became women, some of them healers and visionaries for their tribes and villages.

RELATIONSHIP CHANGES

Many girls experience changes in their relationships with others around the time of their first moon. You might notice that this time brings you closer to the women in your life. Having your first moon is something you can share with other girls and women — such as your friends, older sisters, mom, aunts, and grandmothers. But it is also a time when you might want more privacy or space from your mom or older sisters, and from your brothers or dad.

Sometimes girls sense that their parent or parents now treat them a little differently — like more of a grown-up. Parents can have mixed feelings about watching their daughters grow up. Mostly, parents feel full of love and happiness for their daughters, but they can also feel some sadness at seeing their little girls change into young women, just as they felt both joy and sadness when they watched them grow from babies into toddlers and from toddlers into little girls. Sometimes parents, especially fathers, want to be respectful of this amazing change in your life, and so they give you more space. This might be great, or it might be difficult.

Dads often try hard to act casual with their daughters about all these changes, but because a girl's changes are different from a boy's, they might not always say or do the best thing. Sometimes they need a little educating. If you think this is the case with your dad, you can talk to him about it, give him a book like this one, or ask him to talk to your mom or aunt about it.

You also might notice that you have new feelings for or attractions to your classmates. Maybe you have a crush on a kid in your class; whenever they're around, you feel happy or shy or both. This change, too, is normal, expected, and part of growing up. The best approach you can take is to just relax and try to enjoy these new feelings as much as possible. It's also good to pay attention to and respect all the feelings you have and to let the people around you know about them.

GIRL TIME

"Girl time" is important and a lot of fun. It's a time to hang out and share first-moon stories and tales about other life experiences with your mom, other moms, aunts, sisters, and friends, and it's part of what makes being a girl so interesting and unique.

Being able to share your experiences, accomplishments, fears, and worries with other girls and women, and hearing stories about their experiences with moontime and coming of age, is a great way to learn the secrets of self-care. It's also super-fun to hear about all the silly stuff girls experience, to laugh and cry about it, to feel understood and offer understanding, and to feel connected. First-moon and coming-of-age stories are common to us all.

Girl time can also include taking walks with your mom or friends, having a slumber party or a girls' day at the beach, or just talking with your women relatives in the kitchen. Typically, girls and women like to gather around something beautiful or creative — for example, we like making a delicious meal together, working on an art project, marching for equality, or taking a hike high on a mountain to see a breathtaking view. You can also meet with other young women specifically to talk about the change you are all going through, to get support, to make friends, and to help one another's dreams come true.

Girls' Circles

Several years ago, my sister Beth realized that she wanted to create a special space for her eleven-year-old daughter, Theresa, so that she could share her experiences in growing up. She wanted it to be a place that Theresa could count as all her own, where she could share with and hear from other girls and women. She also thought it was important that the space include something creative to do and that it be a sacred space, free of gossip and criticism, where girls could speak their minds and hearts, confident that what they shared would not be repeated outside and that they would be supported.

She erected a tent in her backyard and invited five of Theresa's girlfriends to come over for a "girls' circle" once a week for twelve weeks. Each week, the girls focused on a different theme or topic. These included body changes and body image, relationships, goals and dreams, peer pressure, ways to deal with conflicts and communication, and values such as truth telling and fitting in. They also made art projects together, such as collages and life-size pictures of themselves.

Beth, Theresa, and Theresa's five friends loved the group and wanted it to continue, and so it did for the next two years. Each week they shared and listened to one another as they laughed, cried, and safely expressed all the newness in their lives. They supported one another with smiles and strength and beauty. Sometimes they role-played, which means to act out roles in fictional situations, to learn communication skills or ways to handle new situations. For example, role-playing can teach you how to say no to something a friend wants to do but you don't feel good about, or how to ask for something you want but are too afraid to request.

At about the same time, Beth met a woman who lived nearby. She had been doing the same thing with her daughter and daughter's friends. After they met and told each other their experiences, they wanted to share their idea with other girls and moms all over the world, so they created the Girls' Circle Association. Now called One Circle Foundation, it trains moms, "other moms," teachers, juvenile justice workers, and counselors all over North America to facilitate girls' circles. If you are interested in learning about creating a girls' circle for yourself or joining one nearby, go to www.onecirclefoundation.org to learn more.

"My Moontime Experience" by Fran, 15

The years just before and after I got my period were the worst for me. After that, it was easier, and adolescence seemed to get easier, with not quite so many physical changes happening all at once. I think my best friend, Jennifer, was the biggest help in my life through the hard times. She was my diary and I was hers. No matter if it's your mom, a sister, or a friend, I think every girl needs another female to talk to and relate to during the time of her first period and all through that growing time. It is also important for self-esteem to not be alone in struggles.

I had already started puberty by age ten, and that was hard. At ten I needed a bra, and in my diary I would write about how I knew I needed one but really, really didn't want one. I also didn't want to talk to my mom about it at all. I would become very embarrassed when anything from deodorant to shaving legs to boys to bras came up, and I dreaded those moments.

I was eleven years old, almost twelve, when I got my first period. I was staying at my family's cabin with my aunt and uncle, my sister, and my cousins. On that particular afternoon, the only ones home were my sister Theresa (who is two years older than me) and my younger cousin Mary. I went to the bathroom, and there it was. I was pretty unemotional about it. Probably a little scared and excited and annoyed, but mostly I saw it like it was: my first period, which would be a bit of a hassle from then on.

My sister and cousin were excited and eager to find me some pads and supplies. I remember my cousin exclaimed, "I am so glad I was here for this to happen so it can prepare me." Later, my aunt was excited, too, and she took me aside and told me I could ask for anything. She said that she was proud of me, that it was an exciting time in becoming a woman, and that my mom was coming up to the cabin the next day, so she'd leave the rest to her. I think her words were very sweet and supportive, though I was thinking more about how I hoped no one in the house was listening, and I kept my mouth shut and just nodded and said thank you. It was an embarrassing experience for me.

Nothing embarrassing happened. I just kept worrying about others knowing. Both my mom and I were pretty straightforward about it. You know: "Congrats, here are the pads and tampons, and good luck." I never really thought of it as an honor to my body or as growing up. My mom wanted to celebrate with a dinner or a weekend with her or a girls' night or something, but I thought everything sounded cheesy and unnecessary.

I was frustrated that I could not swim, and this upset me and made my period an annoyance for the first year or even two. I was frightened of tampons for those first periods. I thought the idea of a tampon was incredibly uncomfortable and awkward. I think I was so worried about using tampons that even my body knew, because when I joined the swim team, I planned on not swimming in weeks when I had my period, but the entire season I never got my period once. Once I figured out tampons (and believe me, it took more practice than it should have), I never thought twice about it again, and I always use them.

Being so young and getting my period was part of why I was so reluctant to talk to my mom about it. It seemed so strange to me. Everything about puberty did, and though she offered talks often, I never really talked to her at all about anything. My friends were always the ones I talked to about periods and feeling awkward and all that stuff. After all, they knew exactly what I meant. I do wish I had been able to be more open with my mom about it all, and I think that there isn't much more she could have done to make me that way. It just happened as it did.

MOONTIME JOURNALING
The Journal for the Generations

Besides your moontime journal, you might also want to create another kind of journal, a "journal for the generations." A journal for the generations is a book of your personal stories about being a girl and your first-moon experiences that you can pass along to other women relatives — your younger sister, cousins, nieces, or your own daughter someday. They can read your first-moon reflections, record their own, and pass it along in turn.

You can include anything in the journal that you think would be helpful or interesting for other girls to read. You could write about what it is like to be a girl at this point in history, about your dreams or your experiences during your moontime meditations, and about what your first-moon experience was like.

For centuries, women passed on their wisdom about self-care, menstruation, sexuality, childbirth, healing, and well-being through storytelling. So you might want to interview your grandmothers, mom, sisters, and aunts about their first moons and include their stories in your journal for future generations as well. Hearing the women in your family tell their stories will let you create your own family "herstory," and you can pass on their wisdom for generations to come by hearing and writing down those stories. Even if you find that your mother or grandmothers did not know about or pay much attention to the wisdom of the moontime cycle, you might still find valuable and interesting treasures.

When you interview your mom or your grandmothers, or both, about their first moon, ask how they cared for themselves, what they did/do during their moontimes, and what they might do differently if they could do it all again.

MOONTIME MEDITATION

Generations of Amazing Women

Find a comfortable spot to relax. Close your eyes and take a few breaths. Imagine yourself sitting in the middle of a circle of women. They are all holding hands around you, looking at you with love and admiration. You are happy to be with them in the center of this circle.

As you look more closely at these women, you realize that they are the women of your family — your mother and sisters, your aunts, cousins, and grandmothers. They are also your great-great-grandmothers and their grandmothers. You realize that you are surrounded by generation upon generation of women, all connected to you through your family history. Each woman has her own story, her own dreams, her own sorrows, and her own magic. Now they are sending to you all the lessons they have learned, all their courage, their mistakes and successes, their wisdom and innocence, to support you in living your own dream.

As you imagine the many women who have come before you, feel their strength and power, which live on in you. Now it is your turn to live the life you imagine.

When you are finished, gently open your eyes and move out into the world, confident in the knowledge that many women came before you and that you carry their spirit in your blood and bones, in your mind and heart.

THE IMPORTANCE OF LISTENING
TO YOURSELF AND TO EACH OTHER

Awareness of period stigma continues to grow. In 2017, author Cheryl Strayed and her husband, Brian Lindstrom, produced a video op-ed for the *New York Times* called "I Am Not Untouchable. I Just Have My Period." The video documents their time in Nepal, doing workshops and listening to teenage girls who were students at Kopila Valley School. In Nepalese culture, menstrual taboo is rooted in very old and very ingrained religious beliefs that view girls and women as inferior and the female body as impure. Girls are often banished from their homes during their menstruation, forced to sleep in a cow shed or in the forest, and not permitted to attend school. They are not allowed to eat most foods or to look at their male family members while they're menstruating. The op-ed features local girls talking about the hardships they faced as a result and asking for the discrimination to end. "Fortunately," writes Strayed, "laws have changed, but mindsets must change too. The girls Brian and I met in Surkhet are doing that. With their words and their lives, they're redefining what it means to be female in Nepal. Our most important task is to listen."

MOONTIME MOMENTS
Creating Magic Together

Girls, working together, can create magic. That magic can be as simple as helping a friend feel better by listening to her concerns or as huge as banding together to save the Earth. Create your own magic by having some special "girl time" each week or month.

Make a promise to support one another in life and to help one another remember to take good care of yourselves so that you can all live happy and outrageously magical lives. Read the promise below together, if you like.

Take the Girl Promise

I promise to always treat myself like the amazingly wonderful, gorgeous, brilliant queen that I am. I promise to take time out just for me each month. I promise to go after my dreams. I promise to ask for help when I need it. I promise to love myself more than anything. And I promise to support other girls as they do the same.

Chapter Eleven

CONNECTING TO NATURE

How brave the moon
shines in her skin;
outnumbered by the stars.

— **Angie Weiland-Crosby**

The cycle of the moon is reflected in your body, connecting you to the greater cycles of life, welcoming you into your fullness as a woman.

Just as we are connected to other girls and women by our shared cycle, we are connected to the Earth, moon, sun, and stars around us. The Earth is a living being with cycles and seasons of her own. When we remember that we are part of the natural universe around us, we remember that, likewise, the universe is part of us.

Every morning when I wake up and open my eyes to those first few moments between night and day, when the world is still and quiet, I can feel the Earth alive and ready to give birth to a new day. As the stars fade from view and night gives way, I feel excitement and anticipation at what will happen in the world today.

Sometimes nature surprises me with a breathtaking painting, a sky filled with pinks and purples and rays of golden light. Sometimes I am showered with rain watering my garden, and lightning dances across the sky. Sometimes nature kisses me sweetly with a soft breeze on my face or the warmth of the sun on my skin and the sweet scent of jasmine in the air.

The times when I am out in nature, on my runs or hikes on mountain trails or beside the ocean, are the times I am most at home with myself, the times I am happiest. Nature is where I go to restore myself and dream. The Earth is full of gifts each day. No matter how I feel or what is going on in my life, I can always count on feeling better after I have spent time in the garden or on my runs, seeing, breathing, and feeling the Earth.

NATURE'S MIRROR: THE BUTTERFLY GIRL

I was a caterpillar, happy to be myself. And suddenly I started to feel an inner pulling, some feeling inside that took me away from my life and my world. All I could do was make a room for myself — this small cocoon. I built it around me, soft and warm, so I could dream, though I didn't know of what or why. I decided I couldn't fight it, though I tried, and so I rested, and I dreamed of many things.

When I woke up, I noticed myself changing on the

inside. And for a while I just stayed in my cocoon. But all at once I knew I had to push off and away from my cocoon and open up into the world. And as I did, I noticed that I had changed on the outside, too. I had wings filled with beautiful colors and designs — all unique just to me. And I flew out into the world, happily dancing with the flowers, enjoying their beauty and the beauty of myself.

Like the change from caterpillar to butterfly, your growth from a girl into a woman is a transition filled with new and unfamiliar things. If you listen to your "inner pulling" and care for yourself, you will happily emerge from this time as your beautiful, unique self. Seeing the way nature reflects the many changes we experience in life can be helpful. The more comfortable we are with cycles and seasons — life and death and rebirth, times for turning inward and times for shining in the world — the happier we will be.

MOONTIME AND THE PHASES OF THE MOON

Every month, the moon, like our own bodies, goes through phases. The lunar cycle repeats itself every 29.5 days; the average menstrual cycle lasts about 28 days. In earlier times, before there was electric lighting, women who lived near one another tended to menstruate together on the new, or dark, moon. Just as sunlight and moonlight affect plants and animals, our hormones were triggered by levels of moonlight. Women were aware that their natural cycles happened in synchrony with the moon's phases.

Ancient cultures that celebrated and worshipped goddess figures believed that the goddesses were embodied in the Earth, the universe, and particularly the moon. Moon cycles were seen as reflecting the natural rhythm of a woman's body and life passages. Just as the moon is receptive to the sun's light and reflects that light to Earth, so the energy of the feminine was seen as receptive and reflective.

In Greece, the phases of the moon were given the names of goddesses: Diana for the waxing phase, Selene for the full phase, and Hecate for the waning period. These names mirrored the stages of women's lives: youth, maturity, and old age. The new moon symbolizes beginnings and birth, the waxing moon represents the period from childhood to menarche, and the waning moon mirrors aging and eventually the celebration of menopause.

Science suggests that our body's cycles as well as dreams and emotional rhythms are connected to the moon, the tides, and the planets. The moon and the tides interact with the energy fields of our bodies, and that has an effect on our physical, emotional, and dream lives.

Like the dark phase of the moon, women have times when they need to draw their attention into themselves, and, like the full moon, they have times to shine brightly in the world. Each woman has her own rhythm. The dark moon is the bleeding time, and the full moon is the time of ovulation. Though your own cycle might not exactly follow the phases of the moon, you might find yourself feeling more internal (like the dark moon) while you are bleeding and feeling more external when you are ovulating.

The menstrual cycle, because it connects to the lunar cycle, is a monthly reminder to see how you and all of us are intricately connected to the Earth's greater cycles.

 ## MOONTIME MOMENTS
Tracking the Moon

By tracking the moon in relation to your cycles, you can learn to better understand the variations in your feelings and energy throughout the month.

On the first night of your period, note the phase of the moon. You can track your period and the progress of the moon each month during your period. This will help you compare your personal cycle to that of the moon.

Pay attention to your body and your emotions, and you might notice that you experience the same feelings at around the same time each month. As women, our bodies are aligned with the cycles of the natural world. Making that connection can be a powerful experience.

 ## MOONTIME MAGIC
Plant Your Secret Garden

Gardens are magical places full of new life and beauty. In the garden grow herbs that heal and nourish us, flowers that beautify our lives and give off amazing scents, and vegetables that feed us so that we grow healthy and strong. Creating your own secret garden where you can water and nurture your dreams is a beautiful way to connect with nature.

The fall, when leaves are falling from the trees and the Earth is preparing for her winter sleep, is a perfect time to plant some flowering bulbs. First, get your bulbs (such as tulips or irises), some rich soil, and a planter box or a little spot of earth. You can find a spot in your yard or, if you don't have access to a yard, fill a planter box with soil and keep it outside on your deck, on your windowsill, or at your front door. You might also want some gardening gloves and a small hand shovel (but I like to use my bare hands and get muddy). Ask your parent(s) if they have any bulbs you can use, or go to a nursery and pick out your favorite types of bulbs and the other necessary items.

Bury the bulbs in the rich soil, about three inches below the surface. As you plant them, think of any dream you might have, perhaps something you are working toward during this new school year. Maybe it is a dream of feeling comfortable in your own skin or of being in the school play the following spring. Maybe you dream of being closer to your family or friends. Whatever it is, as you plant your bulbs and care for them over the coming months — watering them when necessary — think of your dream.

Sometimes, when we are preparing for our dreams to come true, we don't think very much is happening. We don't see much changing on the outside or see any results. Sometimes you might think you are doing everything you can, but nothing is happening. But as with the bulb underground, there is a lot going on; it just needs time in the soil before it is ready to enter the world.

Our creative imagination works that way, too. Ideas

need time to grow and take root, to become strong and secure, before they see the light of the sun. Always trust that even if you can't yet see the results, all your dreaming and hard work will soon come to fruition.

When you see the beauty of your garden next spring or summer, when the flowers bloom, remember that you are looking at the beauty and magic of creation that lives inside you. You are seeing and experiencing your own creation, loveliness, and grace.

MOONTIME MEDITATION
Flowering Girl, Flowering Woman

Find a comfortable place to sit on the ground, perhaps in your secret garden. Make yourself comfortable, either lying on the grass or sitting against a tree. Close your eyes. Take some deep breaths into your belly. Just for now, let your day go.

Take in the scents and sounds of the Earth around you. Feel the air on your face. Remember that the oxygen you breathe is created by the Earth's plants and trees and in turn by the sunlight. Take another breath and let everything else on your mind go.

Let yourself melt into the Earth. Feel the Earth below supporting and holding you.

Imagine a root growing from your womb down into the Earth. Like the roots of the strong redwood tree, let your roots grow deep into the soil.

Now imagine the warmth and energy of the Earth traveling up your roots and into your body. Notice how strong you feel when you are connected and rooted to the Earth.

Let the energy travel through your whole body, to the tips of your fingers and toes, up through your belly and throat, and out through the top of your head.

Imagine that your head is like the bud of your favorite flower. As the sun nourishes the flower, let it bloom, opening, petal by petal, up to the blue sky above. Feel the light of the sun as it reaches your flowering head and flows into your body.

Now the energy of the Earth is flowing through your body, connecting you to the soil, grounding you and your visions. The energy of the sun is connecting you to the sky and your spirit; it is sharing your beauty and gifts with the world.

MOONTIME JOURNALING
The Nature of You

Take out your moontime journal. Write about the meditation you just did, then complete the following sentences.

If I were a flower, I would be a _____,
   because…
If I were a tree, I would be a _____,
   because…
I see myself as most like the _____ [ocean,
   sun, sky, Earth, or wind] because…
My favorite thing to do in nature is…
I am grateful for the Earth because…

A Journal Entry by Lizzy, 17

Before I get my period, right in the eye of my personal PMS storm, I have moments when all I want to do is write. The following passage comes from a journal entry I made during such a time, which I later used as part of an essay in college.

The Earth has her own cycles. She cries in the spring, only to see barren trees ripen and turn green. She succumbs to the heat of the summer, cracking and peeling bark off her limbs. Softly shivering in the autumn, she changes colors and slowly sheds layers. In the winter she sleeps naked, covered by city streets, city lights, city buildings, and a blanket of frost, only to wake up again and find insects sipping at her sweet nectar and gently pollinating her petals painted in every hue. The sun rises and falls; the waning crescent moon waxes and is full; the tide is high and then low.

Each of us leads a very different life. But despite these differences, we are all tied to the Earth and her cycles by the flow of energy of our own cycles. We are all born through a body that was brought into this world by another; and we need each other in order to continue in the circle of life.

One day, we will all leave these bodies and continue onward, only to once again become a part of something bigger than these seconds and these minutes, bigger than these days and years.

Life is a gift, a windy road of lessons and speed bumps, stop signs, dead ends, and turnarounds. We begin with the longest short passage we will ever experience in our lives, and we enter the world with a blinded gasp, wriggling and new. We spend our lives trying to figure everything out, not quite knowing what we are searching for but still searching because somebody once told us that there is always something better than this. We laugh and cry; we win and lose; we love hard and fall even harder, only to pick ourselves up, dust ourselves off, and start all over again.

Chapter Twelve

CONNECTING TO YOUR SPIRIT

Look inward — the loving begins with you.
— Oprah Winfrey

Now that you have learned to care for yourself and are taking time for your inner self, you are ready to go out and shine. Like the moon, there are times when you can be hidden from the world and times when you can shine full and bright.

Your spirit is the shining part of you that is strong and unconquerable. Your spirit is whole, perfect, and complete. Your spirit connects you to your talents and dreams, to your visions and inspirations, to nature and your community. Your spirit is you.

MOONTIME HERSTORY
Megan Rapinoe

Megan Rapinoe is a world-class soccer player, who, along with her teammates, delivered the United States a victory by winning the 2019 Women's World Cup!

She is a strong force, on and off the field. An advocate for numerous LGBTQ organizations, she cofounded a gender-neutral lifestyle brand. She is also helping lead the US women's soccer team's fight for equal pay. On International Women's Day, 2019, the national team filed a federal gender-discrimination lawsuit against the US Soccer Federation. The female athletes are seeking pay and treatment equal to that of their male counterparts, as well as damages, such as back pay. Prior to filing this lawsuit, Rapinoe was also part of a group of players who filed a federal labor complaint against US Soccer in 2016, claiming they're paid just 40 percent as much as the men's team players — despite generating tens of millions more in revenue. Clearly, she believes in standing up for herself and making the world a better place! Here are some of her words of wisdom.

I was made exactly the way I was meant to be made in who I am and my personality and the way I was born.

Putting yourself out there is hard, but it's so worth it. I don't think anyone who has ever spoken out, or stood up or had a brave moment, has regretted it. It's empowering and confidence-building and inspiring. Not only to other people, but to yourself.

*What kind of person do you want to be for yourself, but also
in the larger context of the country and in the world?*

— Megan Rapinoe

SEEING SPIRIT IN YOURSELF
AND IN YOUR COMMUNITY

Connecting to our dreams and visions in our community often gives us an opportunity to see our own true spirit, what we are really made of! Maybe one of your dreams is to heal the Earth or to help make period packs for homeless women or to build a better school. By connecting with other people in your school or community to take action and make that dream a reality, you can witness the strength and magic of your spirit in the world.

Kassie's Story

Kassie grew up in a family that did not know very much about caring for the environment. When she was in middle school, her science teacher taught her class about the importance of recycling and how it helps the Earth. Kassie taught her parents about it, and they set up recycling containers in their home.

Kassie and her parents felt good about the fact that, in their own small way, they could help the environment. Kassie continued to learn about caring for the environment and about easy choices people can make to create a healthier Earth. She learned about things that cause pollution and that one of the biggest causes of pollution in the United States is the generation of electricity from coal and fossil fuels. Kassie learned about renewable energy — energy made from sunshine, wind, water, and other nonpolluting natural resources. Using renewable energy to generate electricity made sense to Kassie. Kassie found herself more and more passionate about wanting to make a change for the environment.

When she went to college, she met a girl named Sara, who was also passionate about stopping pollution. Together they started a student movement to get their college to buy electricity made from renewable energy sources instead of polluting energy sources like coal and nuclear power plants. After two years of their hard work, their college became one of the first colleges in the nation to do this. Now many others are doing the same. Today Kassie has a career in renewable energy and trains college students all over the United States in how to get their schools to switch to renewable power.

Kassie followed her interests and her heart and teamed up with another woman, and together they made a major change in their school community to help the Earth. Kassie followed her spirit and is now working in a job she loves, changing the world one college at a time.

MOONTIME MEDITATION
You're a Superstar

Close your eyes. Bring your attention to your heart. Take a few deep breaths. When you are relaxed, imagine you are staring up at a starry sky. Let your eyes wander the sky until you notice a star that is drawing your attention to it. See how it grows brighter and brighter.

Imagine that you and the star are coming closer together — and that now you are filled with the star. It is living in your heart. It is bright and beautiful. Let its warmth fill your body. Let its golden light fill you up and shine out into the room around you. This is you. This is your power and strength and light. This is where all your dreams live. It is your own treasure.

You can play with your star's brightness and decide when you want it to shine brightly in the world for everyone to see and when you want to keep it close inside, just for yourself to smile about. Know that wherever you go, you carry around this beautiful light — you are a superstar.

MOONTIME JOURNALING
If I Could Change the World, I Would

Take out your moontime journal. Imagine and respond to the following scenarios:

1. The leaders of the world have called upon you to be in charge for the year. What are the first five things you'll do? Why?
2. Imagine yourself at the ripe old age of ninety-three. You are a very wise old lady indeed. You have many important words of advice to share with your younger self. You have lived an over-the-top amazing life. Write a letter from

ninety-three-year-old self to yourself today, telling you the five most important things to do during your life.

MOONTIME MOMENTS
Spirit in Action

There is an expression that goes, "Think globally, act locally." This means that maybe there is something you would like to change for the whole world, and that by taking action close to home, you can take the first steps toward making a larger change. Countless other people are working on similar things in their communities. One by one, communities around the world can make big changes that ripple out to the whole world.

How do you get started? Here are some basic steps to follow:

1. **Brainstorm.** Write down one thing you would like to change in your world. Think about others who might be interested in this, too.
2. **Get people together.** Look for people who are interested in and passionate about the same cause and who are willing to commit time and energy to it. Find an adult or organization to help you. You will likely need some of their resources to make your plan a success.
3. **Make a plan.** Set the goals for your project. Write them down clearly, and make sure that every person involved agrees on them. Decide when and

where your group will meet. Make a schedule for the steps of the project. Decide if the project needs money and, if so, how much and how you will raise it. Let people know about the project, and if needed, get permission for everyone to participate.

4. **Put your ideas into action.** Get to work carrying out your plan.

5. **Evaluate what you did.** Together with the other members of your group, write down and respond to the following questions:

    What did we like about our project?
    What would we do differently the next time?

6. **Share your success.** Send thank-you notes and letters of achievement to everyone involved in your work.

7. **Celebrate your success.** When you finish, have an end-of-the-project party. Make special awards for all the participants.

MOONTIME POWER! TOGETHER WE CAN CHANGE THE WORLD!

In 2019, a group of eighth-grade girls from Bronx Prep Middle School in New York worked together to create a podcast entitled *Sssh! Periods.*

They noticed that many students and teachers rarely talk openly about their periods. Many students and teachers still live with "period stigma" that has been passed down from previous generations. On the podcast the girls share their thoughts on why something so natural seems so taboo. "This is a subject that affects everybody in the school because we want to have a comfortable environment for all of us girls," they said in the podcast.

Eighth-graders Kassy Abad, Caroline Abreu, Jasmin Acosta, Ashley Amankwah, Litzy Encarnacion, Raizel Febles, and Kathaleen Restitullo saw the problems and created a podcast to make a difference. Their podcast was submitted by teacher Shehtaz Huq to NPR's Student Podcast Challenge, and they were the Grand Prize Winners at the middle school level!

Not only did they raise awareness about the discomfort and stigma they experienced at school (and, for some, at home), but they also addressed "period poverty," the fact that an estimated 1.1 billion women around the world cannot afford period products; and the "pink tax," which refers to the higher cost of goods for women versus men. Many products marketed to women, such as razors and cleansers, are more expensive than the comparable products for men — even though they are the exact same! The only difference is that they're marketed with pink and other "more feminine" colors and designs.

When girls come together with their shared dreams and visions, they can make real change. These girls acted "locally," and the impact is global. To hear their podcast go to Soundcloud .com and search for *Sssh! Periods*.

MOONTIME MAGIC
Create Your Personal Goddess Box

Find a box or other container that you like — even a shoebox will do! First, bless it with your own personal "goddessness" to make it all your own: Decorate it with stickers, gel glitter pens, and more of your own favorite touches.

Your Goddess Box will be the keeper of your dreams. Every time you think of something you really want, make a wish or say a prayer to your angels, to nature, or to whomever or whatever you pray to, write down that wish, and place the piece of paper in your Goddess Box. I also use mine to hold things I am worried about and don't know what to do about. For example, when I was concerned I would not have enough time to get all my work done along with so many other responsibilities, I wrote on a piece of paper, "Please help! I don't know how to get all this done!" I then let go of my worry and got to work. Over the next couple of days, things shifted. One of my projects was postponed, and a friend offered to take my daughter to the beach for the day so that I could work. Sometimes just putting your wish or concern "out there" by writing it down allows solutions to follow.

For your most special dreams and wishes, dip into your best stationery, or find an extra-pretty bit of paper to write your wish on. Fold it up, seal it with a kiss, and place it in your Goddess Box. Check back by looking into your Goddess Box every few weeks or months to see how your dreams are progressing.

CELEBRATING THE TREASURE INSIDE YOU

It's time to write our own story.

— Misty Copeland

E very girl has a secret. It's the best secret ever. It lives inside her. It is brilliantly bright and beautiful. It is pure happiness.

Every girl is born with a treasure inside, and she has a built-in map for finding it. If she takes care of herself by following her natural cycles and listening to herself and what she needs, she will easily find her hidden gold — and share it with the world.

She can imagine and create amazing things. Girls are gifted with the power to create their heart's desire: a beautiful life and an amazing world. It is in girls' spirits, bodies, and dreams. It is the power of creation.

MOONTIME HERSTORY
Your Secret Treasures

One day I told my girlfriend that I just didn't think there was anything that unique about me. I didn't know what my gifts or my dreams were. She said that I had to start walking around like I had the best secret ever. She told me to smile a secret smile to myself and to other people, and that every time I did so, I should say to myself, "I have a really good secret." I didn't know what she meant. But I tried it, and it made me feel pretty good, so I kept it up.

Now I know what she meant. The secret she talked about is the gift that lives in me and in you. We all carry marvelous secret treasures: our spirit, imagination, dreams, and courage, mixed with the magic of creation.

Now that you have come this far, there's no doubt that you are a shining star. I hope you are celebrating yourself every day, and taking time each month for your own special recognition and retreat. Be good to yourself in all that you do. Dream big, reach high, and take heart in knowing that you are connected to the Earth, the moon, the sun, and the stars. You are connected to the legacy of generations of capable women who have done wondrous things in the world.

It all starts with a little self-care. Trust yourself and remember to ask for help when you need it. Surround yourself with visionary and kind people, with laughter and good friends, with beautiful art and music that make you want to move and groove. While you're at it, be sure to wink at the moon.

If you know yourself and love yourself, you will always be cared for and celebrated each and every day.

I love you to the moon and back again, infinity!

ACKNOWLEDGMENTS

I offer special thanks first and foremost to the great mother goddess for inspiring me with a sweet dream. To my daughter, Chloe: Thank you for being such an inspiration, support, and awesome editor! To my mom, sisters, aunts, grandmothers, and the generations of women that came before me: Thank you for passing on your faith, courage, love, wisdom, and humor. To my nieces and their little ones: Thank you for inspiring me with all your strength and fun and love. To my son, Kai: Thank you for your sweetness, ideas, huge support, and overall amazingness. To Georgia Hughes and Kristen Cashman: For your mad editing skills. And a special thanks to the women and girls mentioned in this book who contributed their heartfelt stories and inspiration — and all the girls who continue to inspire me with their lives each and every day.

A SIMPLE GLOSSARY OF TERMS

biodegradable: Ecologically friendly; will disintegrate naturally into the ground.

cervix: A part of a woman's internal genitalia; the entryway to the uterus.

endometrium: The tissue that lines the uterus.

estrogen: A hormone produced by mature eggs, or ova. Estrogen gives signals for breasts to begin to develop and pubic and underarm hair to grow, along with other, more subtle, changes like making the uterus grow.

external female genitalia: Also known as the vulva, organs of the female reproductive system that you can easily see when you look between your legs; they are located outside the body. These include the labia majora, labia minora, clitoral hood, and clitoris.

feminine hygiene products: Tampons, pads, and other products used to catch menstrual flow.

first moon: Menarche — your first menstruation.

hormones: Chemicals made in the body that tell various organs how to develop and work. The body makes many hormones, and they play a role in almost all puberty changes: growth spurts, breast development, pubic hair growth, skin changes, and menstruation.

hymen: A thin tissue covering the opening to the vagina.

internal female genitalia: The internal organs of the female reproductive system, located inside your body. These include the cervix, uterus, ovaries, and fallopian tubes.

labia majora: The outermost part of the vulva, also called the outer lips.

labia minora: The innermost part of the vulva, also called the inner lips.

medical intuitive: Another term for a healer. Someone who may use alternative techniques for healing, such as visualization and prayer.

menarche: The first onset of menstruation.

menopause: The phase of life when menstruation stops. When a woman reaches a certain age, usually her late forties to early fifties, her ovaries stop producing an egg each month. She no longer has a period or is able to become pregnant.

menses: The three to seven days a month when your body releases menstrual fluid.

menstrual flow: Also known as menstrual fluid, the blood that exits the body during menstruation.

menstrual fluid: Also known as menstrual flow, the blood that exits the body during menstruation.

menstrual protection products: Tampons, pads, and other products used to catch menstrual flow.

menstruation and menstrual cycle: The complete monthly cycle.

moontime: The three to seven days a month when your body releases menstrual fluid.

os: The small opening in the cervix, leading to the uterus.

ova: Also called eggs, these are stored in the ovaries and contain genetic information. After release from the ovaries, if ova are met by sperm, fertilization occurs, resulting in pregnancy.

ovaries: Organs of the female reproductive system that contain the ova, or eggs.

ovulation: The monthly release of a mature egg from an ovary.

period: The three to seven days a month when your body releases menstrual fluid.

pregnancy: Once an egg has been fertilized by a sperm and the fertilized egg has attached itself to the uterine wall, pregnancy has begun. A full-term pregnancy (meaning the baby is fully developed by its end) lasts nine months and results in the birth of a baby.

progesterone: A hormone produced from the sac containing the egg, or ovum, that tells the uterus to thicken its lining and prepare for a possible pregnancy.

puberty: The name for developmental changes, both physical and emotional, that happen between the ages of eight and sixteen. Hormones (chemicals produced by our bodies) cause these changes.

urethra: The very small opening through which your urine passes.

uterus: The womb; the internal organ that holds a pregnancy.

vaginal opening: The beginning of the internal reproductive system. In many girls, the opening is partially covered by the hymen, a thin tissue.

visioning or visualizing: The act of imagining and focusing on a goal during meditation as a way to help bring that goal to life.

vulva: Also known as the external female genitalia, organs of the female reproductive system that you can easily see when you look between your legs; they are located outside the body. These include the labia majora, labia minora, clitoral hood, and clitoris.

SOURCE NOTES

p. 8   *Moontime Mythology: The Goddess Menses:* Adapted from Christiane Northrup, *Women's Bodies, Women's Wisdom* (New York: Bantam, 1998), pp. 147–48.

p. 30   *Moontime Mythology: A Navajo Celebration:* Adapted from Virginia Beane Rutter, *Celebrating Girls: Nurturing and Empowering Our Daughters* (Berkeley, CA: Conari Press, 1996), pp. 110–11.

p. 40   *Moontime Munchies: Many Moons Red Velvet Cupcakes:* Adapted from recipe by Garrett McCord, Simply Recipes, accessed October 14, 2019, https://www.simply recipes.com/recipes/red_velvet_cupcakes_with_cream _cheese_frosting.

p. 62   *Fresh Fruit Facial Cleanser:* Adapted from Cherie De Haas, *Natural Skin Care* (New York: Avery Penguin Putnam, 1987), p. 44.

p. 69   *"The Great Mother Goddess has blessed women":* Shinan Barclay and Mary Dillon, *Flowering Woman: Moontime for Kory (A Story of a Girl's Rites of Passage into Womanhood)* (Sedona, AZ: Sunlight Productions, 1988), pp. 18–19.

p. 104   *"It took me a long time to understand and dissect the words"*: Jill Radsken, "Misty Copeland, Offstage," *Harvard Gazette*, May 10, 2017, https://news.harvard.edu/gazette/story/2017/05/dancer-misty-copeland-shares-her-life-story-with-students.

p. 112   *Moontime Mythology: The Wisdom of Isis:* Adapted from Patricia Garfield, *Dream Catcher: A Young Person's Journal for Exploring Dreams* (Toronto: Tundra Books, 2003), p. 34.

p. 122   *"I can only imagine the amazement and pride my grandparents would feel"*: Teresa Iverson, *Ellen Ochoa* (Chicago: Raintree, 2006), p. 9.

p. 131   *It's easy to "map" your bedroom according to feng shui principles:* Susan Levitt, *Teen Feng Shui* (Rochester, VT: Inner Traditions, 2003). The feng shui decorating suggestions in chapter 9 are adapted from www.susanlevitt.com (accessed 2005).

p. 148   *author Cheryl Strayed and her husband, Brian Lindstrom, produced a video op-ed:* Cheryl Strayed and Brian Lindstrom, "I Am Not Untouchable. I Just Have My Period," *New York Times*, op-ed and film, March 8, 2019, https://www.nytimes.com/2019/03/08/opinion/menstrual-shaming-nepal.html.

p. 168   *"This is a subject that affects everybody in the school"*: "Periods! Why These 8th-Graders Aren't Afraid to Talk about Them," *Morning Edition*, National Public Radio, May 15, 2019, https://www.npr.org/2019/05/15/721729850/periods-why-these-eighth-graders-arent-afraid-to-talk-about-them.

RESOURCES

INFORMATION RESOURCES

The following is a list of helpful body, mind, and spirit resources for girls.

Your Moontime Magic: http://www.yourmoontimemagic .com — This book's companion website, where you can find period essentials such as moontime starter kits, magical moontime mists, free audio meditations (like the ones in this book), free informative videos about all things puberty related, a calendar of events, and links to other resources. Check it out!

Feminist Women's Health Center: http://www.fwhc.org /teens/index.htm

One Circle Foundation: https://onecirclefoundation.org— Information on girls' circles (for ages nine to eighteen).

Our Village Circles: http://ourvillagecircles.com — Offers timely online support circles and empowerment programs, engaging moms of middle schoolers and others to harness collective knowledge and skills for healthy relationships and development in challenging times. Beth Hossfeld, owner and facilitator, is a licensed marriage and family therapist in California and a cofounder of the One Circle Foundation, a national leader preparing adults to provide evidence-based gender-responsive circle programs for youth and families for over twenty years. Visit the website for more information.

PRODUCT RESOURCES

Lola: https://www.mylola.com — Full gamut of menstrual products and information, from first periods to hot flashes!

Diva Cup: https://divacup.com — Eco-friendly and cost-effective menstrual cups.

Lunapads: https://lunapads.com — Washable, reusable pads.

Thinx: https://www.shethinx.com — Period underwear.

Knixteen: https://www.knixteen.com — Period underwear.

The Honest Company: https://www.honest.com — A range of nontoxic, eco-friendly products for body, beauty, and home, including organic cotton tampons.

ABOUT THE AUTHOR

Maureen Theresa Smith is a writer, activist, and communications professional with a background in healing arts. She lives in Marin County, California, and is mom to Kai and Chloe. For her college thesis project, Maureen facilitated adolescent girls' self-esteem circles and researched supporting girls' self-esteem through community action and connection to nature. She continues to host girls' circles and empower girls and women through her writing and one-on-one coaching.

Maureen's life's work has been learning how to integrate spirituality into everyday practices and rituals that are inspirational and fun, in order to support girls and women in becoming whole, strong women. She focuses on offering support and guidance to girls and women as they transition from one phase of life to the next. Her work incorporates a range of healing modalities and fields, including flower essences, aromatherapy, financial planning, support circles, visioning, and life coaching.

Titles by Christine Feehan

MIND GAME
WILD RAIN
SHADOW GAME
DARK SECRET
DARK DESTINY
DARK MELODY
DARK SYMPHONY
DARK GUARDIAN
DARK LEGEND
DARK FIRE
DARK CHALLENGE
DARK MAGIC
DARK GOLD
DARK DESIRE
DARK PRINCE